REGENTS RESTORATION DRAMA SERIES

*General Editor:* John Loftis

MARRIAGE A LA MODE

JOHN DRYDEN

# Marriage à la Mode

*Edited by*

MARK S. AUBURN

UNIVERSITY OF NEBRASKA PRESS • LINCOLN

Copyright © 1981 by the University of Nebraska Press
All Rights Reserved
International Standard Book Number: 0–8032–0386–1
International Standard Book Number: 0–8032–6556–5 (pbk.)
Library of Congress Catalog Card Number: 80–51043

MANUFACTURED IN THE UNITED STATES OF AMERICA

# Regents Restoration Drama Series

The Regents Restoration Drama Series provides soundly edited texts, in modern spelling, of the more significant plays of the late seventeenth and early eighteenth centuries. The word "Restoration" is here used ambiguously and must be explained. A strict definition of the word would be unacceptable to everyone, for it would exclude, among many other plays, those of Congreve. If to the historian it refers to the period between 1660 and 1685 (or 1688), it has long been used by the student of drama in default of a more precise term to refer to plays belonging to the dramatic tradition established in the 1660s, weakening after 1700, and displaced in the 1730s. It is in this extended sense—imprecise though justified by academic custom—that the word is used in this series, which includes plays first produced between 1660 and 1737. Although these limiting dates are determined by political events, the return of Charles II (and the removal of prohibitions against operation of theaters) and the passage of Walpole's Stage Licensing Act, they enclose a period of dramatic history having a coherence of its own in the establishment, development, and disintegration of a tradition.

The editors have planned the series with attention to the projected dimensions of the completed whole, a representative collection of Restoration drama providing a record of artistic achievement and providing also a record of the deepest concerns of three generations of Englishmen. And thus it contains deservedly famous plays—*The Country Wife, The Man of Mode,* and *The Way of the World*—and also significant but little known plays, *The Virtuoso,* for example, and *City Politiques,* the former a satirical review of scientific investigation in the early years of the Royal Society, the latter an equally satirical review of politics at the time of the Popish Plot. If the volumes of famous plays finally achieve the larger circulation, the other volumes may conceivably have the greater utility, in making available texts otherwise difficult of access with the editorial apparatus needed to make them intelligible.

The editors have had the instructive example of the parallel and senior project, the Regents Renaissance Drama Series; they have in fact used the editorial policies developed for the earlier plays as their own, modifying them as appropriate for the later period and as the experience of successive editions suggested. The introductions to the separate Restoration plays differ considerably in their nature. Although a uniform body of relevant information is presented in each of them, no attempt has been made to impose a pattern of interpretation. Emphasis in the introductions has necessarily varied with the nature of the plays and inevitably—we think desirably—with the special interests and aptitudes of the different editors.

Each text in the series is based on a fresh collation of the seventeenth- and eighteenth-century editions that might be presumed to have authority. The textual notes, which appear above the rule at the bottom of each page, record all substantive departures from the edition used as the copy-text. Variant substantive readings among contemporary editions are listed there as well. Editions later than the eighteenth century are referred to in the textual notes only when an emendation originating in some one of them is received into the text. Variants of accidentals (spelling, punctuation, capitalization) are not recorded in the notes except in instances in which they have, or may have, substantive relevance. Contracted forms of characters' names are silently expanded in speech prefixes and stage directions and, in the case of speech prefixes, are regularized. Additions to the stage directions of the copy-text are enclosed in brackets.

Spelling has been modernized along consciously conservative lines, but within the limits of a modernized text the linguistic quality of the original has been carefully preserved. Contracted preterites have regularly been expanded. Punctuation has been brought into accord with modern practices. The objective has been to achieve a balance between the pointing of the old editions and a system of punctuation which, without overloading the text with exclamation marks, semicolons, and dashes, will make the often loosely flowing verse and prose of the original syntactically intelligible to the modern reader. Dashes are regularly used only to indicate interrupted speeches, or shifts of address within a single speech.

Explanatory notes, chiefly concerned with glossing obsolete words and phrases, are printed below the textual notes at the bottom of each page. References to stage directions in the notes follow the admirable system of the Revels editions, whereby stage directions are keyed, decimally, to the line of the text before or after which they occur. Thus, a note on 0.2 has reference to the second line of the stage direction at the beginning of the scene in question. A note on 115.1 has reference to the first line of the stage direction following line 115 of the text of the relevant scene. Speech prefixes, and any stage directions attached to them, are keyed to the first line of accompanying dialogue.

With this volume, the thirty-fifth, the Regents Restoration Drama Series comes to a close. The publishers and the General Editor believe that its purpose—to make available "a representative collection of Restoration drama providing a record of the deepest concerns of three generations of Englishmen"—has been achieved. The Series includes twenty editions of plays written in the seventeenth century, from 1660 through 1700, and fifteen written in the following thirty-seven years. Twelve playwrights—Dryden, Etherege, Wycherley, Lee, Otway, Congreve, Vanbrugh, Farquhar, Cibber, Steele, Fielding, and Lillo—are represented by at least two editions. One edition, Gay's *Beggar's Opera,* also carries musical annotation of the tunes employed.

Our objective of producing a series useful at once to students and to research scholars apparently has been realized. The predictably popular plays have been adopted for classroom use. The importance of the less well-known plays is demonstrated by the inclusion of the titles in selective bibliographies, by the citation of the editions in books and articles, and by the consensus of notices and reviews.

The obligations I as general editor have incurred over the past eighteen years, though warmly remembered, are too numerous to be described. Yet I must thank one person who in certain respects has been my collaborator: Ann Gerike (Robinson) of the University of Nebraska Press, who has skillfully copyedited the Series and not infrequently has tactfully prodded me when I nodded.

JOHN LOFTIS

Stanford University

# Contents

# List of Abbreviations

| | |
|---|---|
| B-B | Lester A. Beaurline and Fredson Bowers, eds. *John Dryden: Four Comedies*. Chicago, 1967. |
| C1 | Collected dramatic works, 1701 |
| C2 | Collected dramatic works, 1717 |
| *OED* | *The Oxford English Dictionary* |
| om. | omitted |
| Q1 | First quarto, 1673 |
| Q2 | Second quarto, 1684 |
| Q3 | Third quarto, 1691 |
| Q4 | Fourth quarto, 1698 |
| S.D. | stage direction |
| S.P. | speech prefix |
| Summers | Montague Summers, ed. John Dryden, *Dramatic Works*. Vol. 3. London, 1931. |
| Sutherland | James R. Sutherland, ed. John Dryden, *Marriage à la Mode*. London, 1934. |
| Tilley | Morris Palmer Tilley. *A Dictionary of Proverbs in England in the Sixteenth and Seventeenth Centuries*. Ann Arbor, 1950. |
| *Works* | *The Works of John Dryden*. Gen. eds. Edward Niles Hooker, H. T. Swedenberg, and Alan Roper; textual ed. Vinton A. Dearing. Berkeley and Los Angeles, 1956–. |

# Introduction

*Marriage à la Mode* was first published in late May, 1673. During Dryden's lifetime other quarto editions appeared in 1684, 1691, and 1698. Just after his death, the collected dramatic works of 1701 in folio and the collected dramatic works of 1717 in duodecimo, the latter "edited" by William Congreve, included printings of the play. Some modern editors have assumed that Dryden might have had some part in preparing the two editions published not long after his death, but collation shows that he made no changes in *Marriage à la Mode* in these and none in the lifetime quartos after the first. In this century three superior editions of the play, two produced according to modern standards of editorial practice, have offered examples to which this edition is indebted. James R. Sutherland in his modern-spelling edition of 1934 consulted the four lifetime quartos and the folio edition of the dramatic works; Lester A. Beaurline and Fredson Bowers's old-spelling edition examined as well the 1717 duodecimo, as did Vinton A. Dearing's old-spelling edition in the California Dryden.[1] Every serious modern version, including this edition, has chosen as copy-text the first quarto.

The present edition is based upon collation of copies of the four separately published quartos, and of the folio and the duodecimo of the dramatic works. This collation reconfirms earlier findings that the lifetime quartos after the first were each based on the most recently published edition and that the two collected editions independently returned to the first quarto of 1673 for copy-text. The collation revealed no stop-press variants among the formes of the editions after 1673; the ten copies of the

---

[1] James R. Sutherland, ed., *Marriage à la Mode* (London, 1934); L. A. Beaurline and Fredson Bowers, eds., *John Dryden: Four Comedies* (Chicago, 1967), pp. 277–363; *Works*, 11(1978, ed. John Loftis, David Stuart Rodes et al.): 219–316; Rodes is the principal author of the commentary on *Marriage à la Mode*, pp. 460–505. Vinton A. Dearing in the textual notes *(Works,* 11:601–613) provides the most comprehensive summary of the seventeenth- and eighteenth-century textual history.

first quarto consulted, only one of which had been recorded as used in previous editions, confirmed one set of the two sets of stop-press variants recorded in modern authoritative editions and offered no variants, substantive or accidental, that could not be attributed to deviations in inking or impression.[2] The copy-text for this edition is the 1673 quarto owned by the Ohio State University Library.

In modernizing the spelling and punctuation, I have chosen to italicize consistently and to spell in their modern manner those French words which Melantha and her interlocutors speak, with certain exceptions. When the first quarto does not italicize and I do, I cite my authority in the textual notes; and when I choose not to italicize words for which I think Dryden might have intended French pronunciation, I cite them in the explanatory notes.[3]

The textual notes provide full explanation for most decisions and emendations; however, one editorial choice that takes issue with the two modern old-spelling editions deserves brief discussion. In all early editions, Polydamas's dead wife is called "Eudoxia" at I.378, 383, 386 and "Eudocia" at III.i. 399, 400, 403. For no stated reasons, Bowers emends the latter appearances to "Eudoxia," Dearing the earlier to "Eudocia." The name appears variously as "Eudoxia" and "Eudoxa" in John Fletcher's *Valentinian* (1612) and Philip Massinger's *The Emperor of the East* (1631), and it was emended by Massinger's nineteenth-century editor to "Eudocia" and Fletcher's twentieth-century editor to "Eudoxa." In Dryden's play, I base my decision not to emend on the absence of clear orthographic preference in earlier French and English literature and on pronunciation. Scansion suggests that on its first appearances a tetrasyllabic pronunciation (*you-DOCKS-ee-AH*) reads better than the trisyllabic pronunciation (*you-DOE-sha*),

---

[2] Beaurline and Bowers as well as Dearing record "concerment" for "concernment" on the inner forme of sheet F and two variants on the inner forme of sheet K. Copies from the Folger, the Huntington, the Indiana University, and the Ohio State University libraries were corrected in both formes; copies from the Newberry, the Yale University (2), the University of Chicago, and the University of Texas libraries, as well as a second from the Folger Library, were corrected in sheet K and uncorrected in sheet F.

[3] For a compact discussion of Dryden's use of French words, see E. A. Horsman, "Dryden's French Borrowings," *Review of English Studies*, n.s. 1 (1950): 346–351.

which is preferable for the same reason in the name's second appearances.

Although *Marriage à la Mode* was not published until mid-1673, it was probably first performed by the King's Company of players in late November, 1671.[4] In all likelihood, Dryden had completed the play earlier that year, for Rochester had "commended it to the view of His Majesty, then at Windsor" (Dryden writes in his dedicatory epistle), some time between May 27 and July 13, 1671. On November 9, the rival Duke's Company opened a splendid new theater in Dorset Gardens, "nearer home" to the city of London and possessed of intricate modern stage machinery to present, as Dryden notes sarcastically in his Prologue, "gay shows and gaudy scenes." For their first production the younger company revived Dryden's four-year-old farce, *Sir Martin Mar-all*; the competitive situation makes likely the older King's Company's answering with a new play by Dryden, their shareholder and major playwright. Two later events tend to confirm a late November opening. Certainly by December 14 and probably by December 7 the King's Company offered Buckingham's burlesque, *The Rehearsal*. The play attacks Dryden in the character of Bayes; and while the most direct verbal allusions are to Dryden's *The Conquest of Granada* (in two parts, December 1670 and January 1671), contemporary comment and recent careful study suggest hits against the romantic heroic plot of *Marriage à la Mode*.[5] On January 25, 1672, the King's Company's theater in Bridges Street was totally destroyed by fire. The company lost everything, and if Dryden's tragicomedy had opened in the Duke's Company's old theater in Lincoln's Inn Fields, where the King's Company played between February 26, 1672, and March 26, 1674, we would expect a different comparison between the two companies in the Prologue.

The King's Company cast its strongest actors in the comic roles.

---

[4] Earlier conjectures, based on the Prologue's allusions to the Third Dutch War (declared March 17, 1672, but preparations must have begun earlier), were for a late March or early April, 1672, opening. But Robert D. Hume in "The Date of Dryden's *Marriage A-la-Mode*," *Harvard Library Bulletin*, 21 (1973): 161–166, has shown the late November date to be more probable. *Works*, 11: 460, accepts Hume's argument.

[5] *A Key to The Rehearsal* (1704) suggests some similarities; Rodes, in *Works*, 11: 462–464, details several grounds of parody.

Charles Hart performed Palamede. The lover of the promiscuous Lady Castlemaine was clearly the leading actor of the organization and later would have the roles of Wycherley's Horner and Manly. Little Major (Michael) Mohun played Rhodophil, probably with great military dignity. Separately they took the prologue and epilogue, those performing gems coveted by the best actors. Each had acted before the Restoration, and Mohun was certainly in his fifties; but audiences demanded no correlation between a male character's age and that of his impersonator.

Actresses were less lucky, for audiences expected in young female characters the bloom of youth and the figure of seventeen, particularly in the titillating breeches roles, one of the few opportunities outside the bedchamber where the shape of a female calf and thigh might be examined. Rebecca ("Beck") Marshall, as notable for her real-life sexual intrigues as for her dark-haired beauty and stage presence, could have brought to Doralice a certain imperiousness typical of her usual role as passionate heroine. Nell Gwyn seems the obvious choice for the great comic role of Melantha, but her petite figure, made so famous beneath the broad-brimmed hat she wore for her celebrated monologues, was swollen with the royal bastard she would deliver on Christmas Day, 1671, and the character was played by Elizabeth Boutell, famous for her fair purity. If Dryden had written Melantha for Betty Boutell (and we may be sure he knew the capacities of his company), we would expect more naïveté and innocence than many readers of the play are willing to grant this female fop; perhaps, then, he did originally write the part for little Nell. Whether Dryden intended the role of Philotis, Melantha's cunning servant, for Anne Reeves, called "Mrs. Reeve" in the cast list (and whether Anne Reeves was indeed Dryden's mistress), we can only speculate.

Complementing the witty lovers of the comic line of action were competent actors in the romantic roles. Though not the stars of the company, they brought experience and ability to their parts. As Leonidas, delicately handsome Edward Kynaston probably offered majesty, imperious vivacity, and romantic tenderness. How Elizabeth Cox performed as Leonidas's dear Palmyra we cannot be sure. She was new to the company and appears to have been steered toward such comic roles as Violetta in *The Assignation* (1672) and such serious roles as Desdemona in a revival (1674?) of

*Othello.* (Offstage Betty Cox too, like Beck Marshall and Nell Gwyn, achieved a certain notoriety, however spotless she was on the boards.) William Wintershall as Polydamas and Edward Lydall as Argaleon have left few clues beyond their previous roles as heroic villains to tell us of their distinctive abilities.[6]

✓ The casting of strong actors in the comic roles and less powerful ones in the romantic roles reflects the nature of the play itself. Like Dryden's best tragicomedies, *Marriage à la Mode* has a double plot in which two sets of characters interact only in the most casual way. Rhodophil is captain of the king's guard, Palamede a hopeful courtier, Doralice a lady-in-waiting, and Melantha a would-be court lady; but except for Melantha's unfortunate impertinence to Palmyra (V.89–129), the comic characters never enter the world of the romantic heroic characters except in such noncomic and trivial ways as do not significantly affect the romantic action and affect the comic action inconsequentially. Each line of action largely moves independently of the other, materially and efficiently, to its conclusion. Two critical problems arising from this structural pattern concern unity of tone and unity of action.

✔ Dryden's great Renaissance predecessors Shakespeare, Beaumont, and Fletcher had all written plays which ignored unity of tone and mingled serious with comic plots; and if Dryden's Lisideius in *Essay of Dramatick Poesie* found "mirth and compassion. . . incompatible" and "*English* Tragi-comedie" "absurd," his Neander thought that "a Scene of mirth mix'd with Tragedy has the same effect upon us which our musick has betwixt the Acts."[7] Where critics (particularly those influenced by such French formalists as Rapin, as was Lisideius) might carp, audiences paid their way to performances, and eighty years later Dr. Johnson would still assert "that the tragic and comic affections have been

---

[6] In the three previous paragraphs I am indebted to several earlier studies: John Harold Wilson's groundbreaking book, *All the King's Ladies: Actresses of the Restoration* (Chicago, 1958); Philip H. Highfill, Jr., Kalman A. Burnim, Edward A. Langhans, eds., *A Biographical Dictionary of Actors, Actresses, Musicians, Dancers, Managers & Other Stage Personnel in London, 1660–1800*, 16 vols. projected (Carbondale, Ill., 1973—); and Rodes in *Works*, 11: 547–557.

[7] *An Essay of Dramatick Poesie* in *Works*, 17 (1971; ed. Samuel Holt Monk, A. E. Wallace Maurer et al.): 35, 46.

moved alternately with equal force, and that no plays have oftner filled the eye with tears, and the breast with palpitation, than those which are variegated with interludes of mirth."[8]

But if disunity of tone could achieve superior effects, disunity of action posed more problems. "It is necessary that of every play the chief action should be single," wrote Johnson long after the neo-Aristotelianism of Thomas Rymer's *Tragedies of the Last Age Considered* (1677) had caught and held the attention of English critics; "for since a play represents some transaction, through its regular maturation to its final event, two actions equally important must evidently constitute two plays."[9] Dryden was certainly aware of the strictures against double plots. He asserted in the dedication to *The Spanish Friar* (1680) that in the play he had "satisfied" his "humour, which was to tack two plays together; and to break a rule for the pleasure of variety."[10] And in *Marriage à la Mode*, as in his other tragicomedies, Dryden's carpentry followed from another principle at least as important to the increasingly accepted body of critical theory to which he added so much both by practice and by precept: decorum.

Decorum prescribed that characters of highest rank should speak and conduct themselves according to their station: their sentiments should be exalted, their actions noble and circumspect. Only characters from lower ranks (persons of high social state, but not princelings) would be capable of wit, repartee, and comic sexual intrigue, only persons of the meanest ranks of mere buffoonery. Villains within the noble circle, often imposters, would expose themselves by their failure to maintain decorum, as Argaleon does by his sarcasm and Polydamas by his treachery. If, therefore, Dryden wished to lighten his heroic feasts with a course of mirth or to introduce a serious main dish in his banquet of witty conversation, he must perforce make his romantic heroic

[8] Samuel Johnson, *Rambler* #156, in *The Yale Edition of the Works of Samuel Johnson*, ed. Allen T. Hazen and John H. Middendorf (New Haven, 1958–), 5 (1969; ed. W. J. Bate and Albrecht B. Strauss): 69.

[9] Johnson, *Works*, 5: 69.

[10] Dedication to *The Spanish Friar* in *The Works of John Dryden*, ed. Sir Walter Scott, rev. George Saintsbury, 17 vols. (Edinburgh, 1882), 6: 409. Indeed, in *The Grounds of Criticism in Tragedy*, prefixed to *Troilus and Cressida* (1679), Dryden asserts of *Marriage à la Mode* that "there are manifestly two actions, not depending on one another" (Scott-Saintsbury, 6: 260).

and comic characters "*well chosen, and kept distant from interfearing with each other*" "*as if they were Mountagues and Capulets.*"[11] Indeed, Dryden took it as a fault in *Secret Love* (1667) that his comic lovers, Celadon (Charles Hart) and Florimell (Nell Gwyn), humorously discussed their marriage at the conclusion of the play in the presence of the Queen of Sicily.[12] In such a situation she could only stand mute: decorum in characterization proved a more important principle than unified dramatic action. Dryden maintained decorum in his more successful tragicomedies by the simple expedient of separating the characters and their lines of action completely, despite the lack of unity of action. And when, at the conclusion of *Marriage à la Mode*, Melantha would force her impertinent if amusing addresses upon the now-recognized king Leonidas, her threat to decorum is ended in four aside speeches between her and Palamede.[13]

In examining the two lines of action in *Marriage à la Mode*, therefore, perhaps we can expect our discussions to sound like those of two different plays. Indeed, the sources for the two plots are radically different—and sources there are, for Dryden, like Shakespeare, thought it no plagiarism to mold the work of his predecessors to his present needs: "what would be theft in other Poets, is onely victory in him," Dryden wrote of Jonson's borrowing.[14] If the comic plot is suggested by Molière and others, the romantic heroic plot springs directly from Madeleine de Scudéry's tale of "Sesostris and Timareta," part of her sprawling romance *Artamène: ou le Grand Cyrus.*[15] Like Shakespeare dealing

[11] Preface to *An Evening's Love* (1668), in *Works*, 10 (1970; ed. Maximillian E. Novak and George Robert Guffey): 206; then Lisideius in *An Essay of Dramatick Poesie*, in *Works*, 17: 35.

[12]. Preface to *Secret Love*, in *Works*, 11 (1966; ed. John Loftis): 117.

[13] For my discussion of Dryden's intentional use of double plotting in his tragicomedies, I am indebted to John Loftis's essay, "Dryden's Comedies," in *Writers and Their Background: John Dryden*, ed. Earl Miner (London, 1972), pp. 27–57, esp. pp. 38–41.

[14] *An Essay of Dramatick Poesie*, in *Works*, 17: 49.

[15] Gerard Langbaine first named the source in his testy *An Account of the English Dramatick Poets* (1691). See also Ned Bliss Allen, *The Sources of John Dryden's Comedies* (Ann Arbor, 1935), pp. 261–268, and Rodes in *Works*, 11: 467–469, for a fuller account. The romance was published in Paris, 1651, and first appeared in English translation from 1653 to 1655. "Sesostris and Timareta" appears in part VI, books 2 and 3, part VII, books 1 and 2.

with similar materials, Dryden condenses the narrative to a more rapidly paced dramatic action covering three days, ties the exposition of character to action, and gives increased emphasis to the role of the younger villain, Heracleon (Argaleon), in order that he may serve as foil to his hero, Leonidas. He retains the pastoral nurture of the young hero and heroine, the torn letter to confuse their identities, and the usurpation of the throne; in the only clear verbal allusion, Leonidas and Palmyra, like Sesostris and Timareta, are called "miracles."[16] One major difference in the action occurs: Scudéry's Sesostris regains his throne from Amasis when the usurper is overcome with guilt, but Dryden's Leonidas wrests his birthright by force from an unrepentant Polydamas.

A twentieth-century playreader finds tales like Scudéry's and Dryden's vaguely distasteful. A usurping king, an ambitious evil heir-apparent, mysterious but seemingly near-perfect youth and maiden with first a fear of incest about them and later a natural love so pure it could only have been made in the ether; all this coupled with robbers, dissembling but honest advisers, jewels and letters substituted for proper identity papers and then delivered only at the crucial times, a noble sister whose misplaced love can only bring misfortune to all, and wild swings of fortune that send one scale plunging while another mounts: such fanciful characters, situations, and devices smack of the spectacular, or the self-satiric, or the merely ideational; they seem devoid of psychologically verisimilitudinous characterization or naturalistically probable action.[17] Yet stories of this nature continue to bring pleasure to countless millions in a form more familiar to us. An enslaved princess is beloved by the captain of her captors' guards; he in turn is beloved by his king's daughter: despite the conflict of love, honor, and duty, he remains faithful to his slave girl, though mutual death is the conclusion of their love. A noble

---

[16] Dryden himself asserted that his adaptations contained few verbal borrowings: *"I seldome use the wit and language of any Romance or Play which I undertake to alter"* (Preface to *An Evening's Love,* in *Works,* 10: 211).

[17] Although many recent studies have emphasized the ideas dramatized in Restoration heroic drama, some defenders suggest that the plays themselves were designed to satirize their own genre, or to poke fun at the audience's satisfaction with heroic plays. But as Robert D. Hume, *The Development of English Drama in the Late Seventeenth Century* (Oxford, 1976), p. 191, points out, if that were so, "why was *The Rehearsal* written"?

lady is tricked by means of a forged letter into believing her brother's bitterest enemy does not truly love her, reluctantly marries her brother's choice, and is driven mad when her lover proves his faith: suicide and insanity follow. The form is, of course, grand opera: the brief synopses sketch the plots of Guiseppe Verdi's *Aida* and Gaetano Donizetti's *Lucia di Lammermoor.* Unlike Dryden's story they end unfortunately, but in common with it they share characters whose perceived psychological depth depends upon acceptance of nonnaturalistic conventions, situations and devices improbable by modern standards of verisimilitude, conflicts of love, honor, and duty, inflated rhetoric, and spectacle. They are not self-satiric, and they are not merely plays of ideas—despite Wagnerian "philosophy." Their appeal depends upon a common agreement by the audience to be moved by certain accepted principles of situation and character—romantic, exalted, probable only within the constraints of the genre.[18]

That Dryden sought to arouse "admiration, compassion, and concernment" through romantic heroic plots like that of *Marriage à la Mode* cannot be doubted.[19] Despite the low humor of *The Assignation* (1672), Dryden seemed to be "pulling away from a literal concept of the representation of nature in drama and moving toward a more imaginative and antirealistic one" in the late 1660s and early 1670s.[20] In such an antirealistic plot Amalthea's artificial scene of exposition to Artemis (I.256–314) should bother us no more than Prospero's long-winded history lesson to Miranda *(The Tempest,* I.ii.16–184) and the vicissitudes of Leonidas's and Palmyra's fortunes no more than those of the victims of "love-in-idleness" in *A Midsummer-Night's Dream.* Our

---

[18] Hume, *Development of English Drama,* pp. 226–229, discusses the comparison of heroic drama in general to grand opera and refers to the many previous critics who have made it. See particularly Eric Rothstein, *Restoration Tragedy* (Madison, 1967), p. 184, who also suggests that we try to imagine seeing the film of *Gone with the Wind* without knowledge of the motion picture romance genre.

[19] Robert D. Hume, in his analysis of Dryden's critical principles as expressed in the *Essay of Dramatick Poesie* and its "Defence," identifies these affective purposes. See *Dryden's Criticism* (Ithaca, 1970), pp. 199–202.

[20] Hume, *Dryden's Criticism,* p. 203. See also Loftis, "Dryden's Comedies," on the "fairy tale quality [of] the dynastic complications[,] . . . a remoteness from historical reality" (p. 47).

pleasure lies in seeing how the poet manipulates generically familiar materials—characters, situations, ideas. How will this recitative surprise, that aria move, that duet please? As music and spectacle turn melodrama into high art in the opera, so does the poet, ever present behind his stereotypical characters and story, make romance memorable.[21]

Dryden's first choice was to make his romance a pastoral. Setting the play in Sicily (a choice which by no means prevents our perceiving the comic characters as metaphors for Charles's courtiers[22]), he then takes the court into the country on a progress for which Polydamas "best knows the reason" (I.104). There Dryden can display the natural dignity of his romantic hero and heroine, by birth associated with the nobility but by nurture with the idealized countryside. In supple, modulating blank verse, Leonidas belittles the dazzle of the court by comparing it with "The canopy of state spread wide above/ In the abyss of heaven" (I.415–416), expresses his modesty by finding nothing in himself "but what/ Is much above a scorn" (I.427–428), displays his natural imperiousness by rebuking the scornful Argaleon, "You ask too many questions and are/ Too saucy for a subject" (I.439–440). Palmyra, twice called "innocence" and twice "piety," "could be content to be his [Leonidas's] handmaid" (I.459), weeps for his good fortune, asks of time that it pass quickly now and that "to redeem that wrong,/ When he and I are met, be twice as long" (I.480–481). Here, in introducing his romantic lovers, Dryden chooses natural images and simple comparisons. When he presents them alone together for their first duet (II.417–513; one expression of their conflict of love and duty), he shifts to rhymed couplets, nearly all end-stopped, with only three of the forty-seven couplets shared (there is one triplet) and only one line interrupted. Within this artificial,

---

[21] Seeing the poet in the work probably added to the pleasure provided by Restoration heroic drama, just as discerning Puccini's or Wagner's habitual patterns of inventiveness enhances the pleasure of grand opera. Hume, *Dryden's Criticism,* p. 193, argues that Dryden wanted the audience to perceive the poet's hand, to see the play as a conscious artistic contrivance of poetic virtuosity.

[22] Rodes, *Works,* 11: 476, points to three advantages of using this "sun-ripened England": avoiding insults to specific English noblemen; employing non-limiting geographical allusions so that both the pastoral and the witty court language may have full play; taking the court away from the palace.

regulated form he spreads a garland of semi-archaic pastoral images to convey how their love grew and what must follow their separation. Leonidas tends toward the abstract or the metaphysical (lazy slow Love, the tingling kiss, the web-weaving souls), Palmyra toward the rural, pastoral image (maidens drawing lovers' initials in the ashes, the May Day games, the exile to "woods and plains").

The pattern of operatic poetry continues. In the blank verse trio of III.i.276–369, Polydamas (surely a bass) and Leonidas (probably a tenor, though perhaps a baritone) begin by interrupting one another before Polydamas forces his cruel interrogation of Palmyra; the gentle soprano returns to her pastoral images (clustered filberts, talking starling), and her simplicity overwhelms both Polydamas's threat of public scorn and death and Leonidas's exalted abstractions (piety, powers) and vow of suicide ("if sword and poison be denied me,/ I'll hold my breath and die"[23]). With their positions reversed and now Palmyra presumed the royal child, Leonidas closes the act with an aria (one of his two soliloquies in the play; the other is unimportant), employing the standard aggrandizing conceits ("fawning followers," virtues of kingship, "scene enough within") punctuated by an almost blasphemous if heroic comparison of himself to the godhead. The mezzosoprano-tenor blank verse duet between Amalthea and Leonidas (IV.i.1–95), all broken and disjointed by her modesty and shame ("failings, sighs, and interruptions") and his angry fury and joyous expectations, makes way for the second duet on love and duty—this one tempestuous—between the lovers (IV.iv.23–105). Once again Dryden chooses rhymed couplets, but this time he breaks them more frequently, particularly in the middle of lines, eschews pastoral images, and except for references to gamesters, a torrent, and a strongbox, nearly always employs abstract imagery. Though ringing changes on well-known bells, the poet joins his sound and sense to surprise and delight, to characterize as expected yet with his own flair, to employ the stereotypical pairings and triplings of characters speaking his own musical language. Surely appreciators of the romantic heroic mode found themselves compelled to admire and pity these characters just as opera lovers see past the absurdities—

[23] See III.i.363–364 n.

considered naturalistically—of grand opera to the beauties within.

The exalted poetry and heroic machinations of these lovers and villains stand toe to toe—buskin to sock—with the witty repartee and breeches intrigue of the four lovers and their clever servant. If we are off in a troubled Elysium with Leonidas and Palmyra, we are in an earthly Cloud Cuckooland with Rhodophil, Palamede, Doralice, and Melantha. Though their setting nominally is Sicily, we recognize them as fashionable members of Charles's court. One is a retainer, one a lady-in-waiting, another a courtier newly returned from travel, the fourth an absurdly amusing would-be court lady. Each is young, physically attractive, rich, witty, and more or less leisured; they are perfect candidates for flirtation, assignation, and sexual intrigue, the cloth from which we expect a comedy of manners to be cut.

But in fact the pattern by which we know high Restoration comedy best had not yet been designed. Of the eight best plays of Etherege, Wycherley, and Congreve, only *She Would If She Could* (1668) had been performed before *Marriage à la Mode*. The late 1660s saw a spate of French-influenced city farces and lightened Spanish romance intrigues: Etheregean comedy was hardly a rivulet before this flood.[24] Dryden was aware that even his own work—by which he probably had in mind *Sir Martin Mar-all*—had descended *"from Comedy to Farce,"* to *"forc'd humours, and unnatural events, . . . what is monstruous and chimerical."* He approved *"most the mixt way of Comedy; that which is neither all wit, nor all humour, . . .neither all cheat . . . nor all adventure."* He wanted to achieve *"repartie in particular; as it is the very soul of conversation, so it is the greatest grace of Comedy, where it is proper to the Characters."*[25] If *Marriage à la Mode* be raised "beyond the ordinary lowness of my comedies," writes Dryden in his dedicatory epistle to Rochester, then copying the "conversation," "the gallantries of courts, the delicacy of expression, and the decencies of behavior" of Roches-

[24] For a fuller discussion of theatrical trends and conditions in the late 1660s, see Hume, *Development of English Drama*, pp. 233–268, and esp. pp. 274–275.
[25] Preface to *An Evening's Love*, in *Works*, 10: 203, 206. Loftis, "Dryden's Comedies," pp. 38–39, quotes these passages in context to show Dryden's conscious attempt in *Marriage à la Mode* to achieve a higher comedy.

ter and other "true wits" is responsible, not just conjoining a comic with a romantic heroic plot.[26]

Indeed, we most frequently remember these comic characters for their witty language. Each encounter marks a fresh battle of wills carried out by means of a verbal duel. Their wit is characterized not only by *double entendre* and puns, but also by striking comparisons among apparently dissimilar things. The foci of these image groups were venerable vehicles even by Dryden's time: the love game is compared to hunting and sport, the sexual negotiations to legal, commercial, theological, and international treaties and governance, sexual desire to appetite for food or drink. As frequently as not, the tenor of the metaphor masks itself in a form Jeremy Collier found smutty or blasphemous. The triangular proviso scene among Rhodophil, Palamede, and Doralice (V.306–394) brings all the threads together: the game of "hide and seek," the "delicate screwed gun" for the hunt; indentures, leagues, a "blessed community," faith as the basis for love and religion; jealousy as "the most delicate sharp sauce to a cloyed stomach," a *ménage à quatre* as a dinner made impossible since both women would "be wishing the longest cut" of the "standing dish." Just as poetic invention within fixed parameters characterizes the art of the romantic heroic plot, so witty conversation with lively new turns on familiar topics marks the comic plot.

For Melantha, language is both the means and the matter of characterization. Founded most likely upon the title characters of Molière's *Les précieuses ridicules* (1660),[27] she reflects in excess the fashionable preoccupation with things French in Charles's court during the first decades after his return from exile. In the "Defence of the Epilogue" (1672) appended to the second part of *The Conquest of Granada,* Dryden rallied at "those Fopps, who . . . pretend they cannot express their meaning in *English,* because they would put off to us some *French* phrase of the last

[26] See Hume, *Development of English Drama,* p. 277, on Dryden's attempt to mimic "fine conversation."

[27] Rodes, in *Works,* 11: 470–471, cites Molière's play along with several other sources, most notably a "ubiquitary" lady from *Artamène: ou le Grand Cyrus* suggested by Leslie Howard Martin, Jr., *Philological Quarterly,* 52 (1973): 746–753.

Edition."[28] Melantha, with her culled lists and eagerness to lead a fashion, embodies his scorn. Yet he was most careful to maintain a charm and a dignity in her, raising her above a Jonsonian "humours" character and endowing with humanity what another author might have left two-dimensional. Beautiful and rich, Melantha is sycophant and fop; eccentric and Francophile, she also enjoys real friendship with Doralice and Artemis (see how gently they handle her in III.i.103–197); and if she must undergo frustrating comic reproof by Palamede (V.89–194), she nonetheless fascinates both young men and might indeed change the court to her humor, as Palamede predicts (V.525–529). In her we see on the one hand her successors Sir Fopling Flutter and Sir Novelty Fashion, on the other Harriet, witty Angelica, and lovely Millamant in full sail.[29]

The plot in which these four lovers are involved follows naturally from the witty song about the inclinations of sexual appetite that opens the play.[30] Its antimatrimonial message reveals the mood of all four comic protagonists and promises a search for fresh stimulation in extramarital affairs. Thereafter, in scenes alternating with the events of the romantic heroic plot, we meet the young lovers and see their efforts to pair off. Dryden uses two sorts of scenes, expository and impelling. The first kind introduces and develops the characters, or involves them in somewhat predictable but delightful self-contained set pieces, or sparks conflicts which further the action only slightly. Thus early in Act II we meet Melantha and, having experienced a firsthand taste of

[28] "Defense of the Epilogue," in *Works*, 11: 211.

[29] James Sutherland, *English Literature of the Late Seventeenth Century* (Oxford, 1969), p. 101, calls Melantha Dryden's "finest comic character" in the eyes of most critics. See discussions by Frank Harper Moore, *The Nobler Pleasure: Dryden's Comedy in Theory and Practice* (Chapel Hill, N.C., 1963), pp. 107–109; Rodes in *Works*, 11: 470–471, 482; and Bruce King, *Dryden's Major Plays* (New York, 1966), pp. 87–90, who sees Melantha's fopperies as "armaments in her battle" for Hobbist "glorification" (p. 87). Margaret Lamb McDonald, *The Independent Woman in the Restoration Comedy of Manners* (Salzburg, 1976), briefly examines Melantha's relationship to the précieuse figure, pp. 52–58.

[30] The relationship of the songs to the play deserves further study. William Myers, *Dryden* (London, 1973), p. 57, argues that this song, like "While Alexis lay pressed" (IV.ii.47–67) is associated with the romantic heroic characters (Amalthea told Doralice to learn "Why should a foolish marriage vow") and sees a tension between the purity of Leonidas's pastoral love for Palmyra and the sophistication of Restoration life.

her humor, watch her absurdities with Palamede in an expected meeting which changes neither's intentions; later we have such expository scenes as Rhodophil and Doralice's domestic argument, Artemis and Doralice's discussion with Melantha about court, town, and country life, Melantha's practice session with her word list, and Philotis's extortion of Palamede.[31] Despite their essentially static nature, these expository scenes please us through their wit and situations. In the impelling scenes the complications initiated by character development bear fruit. Dryden uses essentially the same technique four times: will the identities and the intentions of the potentially adulterous be revealed to the potentially injured? Thus Palamede nearly exposes to Rhodophil his lust for Doralice (II. 124–154), Doralice and Palamede are caught in the middle of "hide and seek" (III.ii.66–155), the masquerading "boys" and their friends need to keep their identities secret, especially after Rhodophil's re-entry (IV.iii.84–196), and Rhodophil interrupts Doralice and Palamede's *tête-à-tête* (V.306–394). In the epilogue Dryden has Rhodophil remind the audience that "each design fell short" because he repeatedly "came in to break the sport" just as consummation seemed inevitable. The mild comic anxiety evoked by the potential discoveries during conversations and assignations moves the action almost episodically to its predictable conclusion, the ultimate confrontation between the belligerent male lovers. Luckily, Doralice the peacemaker has a cooler head and better persuasive powers than her husband and her "servant": the young men reach a happy, mutually satisfactory accommodation which, though it is an emotional necessity given our consistently comic expectations and concern for all, is in no way a necessary consequence of the foregoing action.

The decision to recognize and accept matrimonial fidelity and to abjure fresh external stimulation springs not from the characters' genuine commitment to marital chastity but from the playwright's need to end his action happily. That each woman is attractive by virtue of her power to attract a different man, and hence more desirable to her rightful lover, both Rhodophil and Palamede were capable of knowing as early as Act II. But the play

---

[31] Rodes in *Works*, 11: 473, notes that this last, conventional scene is a variation on a similar one in *An Evening's Love*, the play of Dryden's most like *Marriage à la Mode*.

does not conclude until all the potential fun of the situation has been extracted.[32] What, then, is the relationship of the artificially concluded comic action to the issues of promiscuity and marital fidelity? Critics have seen it as an attack on antimatrimonial plays, as a "witty plea for the validity of married love," as an assault on the audience's own loose morality masked in flattery and frivolity, as an attempt ironically to make marital fidelity "the fashion instead of adultery," even as an "impassively lewd" piece whose author greets marriage "with at the best an uneasy and mistrustful acquiescence."[33] Contemporaries were split: on the one hand Dryden could be cited in a pamphlet of 1674 as one who celebrated marriage and married love; on the other his play could be assailed in a comedy of 1673 as one of the antimatrimonial mode.[34] Perhaps the best answer is that "Dryden refuses to make an emphatic moral judgment" about promiscuity; if he reaffirms the "foolish marriage vow" (I.4) in the conclusion of his comic action, it is "not a very vigorous reaffirmation, but still an acknowledgement that social anarchy would ensue if matrimonial law should be abandoned."[35]

Earlier I noted that the ties between the comic plot and the romantic heroic plot of *Marriage à la Mode* were tenuous. The characters indeed are related by social station (one set dependent upon the other), and on several occasions the action of heroic

[32] Several critics cite the artificiality of the comic conclusion. See, for instance, George R. Wasserman, *John Dryden* (New York, 1964), p. 78: "The premise on which the comic action of the play rests (that without fresh stimulus, marriage is a bore) is dropped not because, after examination, it is found to be unsatisfactory, but simply to bring the action to a close after the comic value of its premise has been exhausted."

[33] John Harrington Smith, *The Gay Couple in Restoration Comedy* (Cambridge, Mass., 1948), p. 70; John Harold Wilson, *Preface to Restoration Drama* (1965; rpt. Cambridge, Mass., 1968), p. 127; A. N. Okerlund, "Dryden's Joke on the Courtiers: *Marriage A La Mode*," *Seventeenth-Century News*, 34 (1976): 5–7; Moore, *Nobler Pleasure*, p. 105; Donald Bruce, *Topics of Restoration Comedy* (London, 1974), p. 152.

[34] Rodes, *Works*, 11: 484–485, cites and discusses the pamphlet *Marriage Asserted;* Hume, *Development of English Drama,* p. 292, shows that Joseph Arrowsmith's *The Reformation: A Comedy* attacks both the heroic and the comic plots of Dryden's play. Hume stresses the irony of Dryden's contributing through his play to the bawdry he deplored in the farcical plays of the late 1660s.

[35] Loftis, "Dryden's Comedies," p. 43.

characters interrupts the games of the comic lovers. But if these *material* ties between the two plots (the relationships of the characters) are somewhat superficial, the *efficient* ties (the extent to which actions influence other actions) are nearly nonexistent. On these grounds *Marriage à la Mode* would seem to lack the organic unity so prized by critics today. But plots within a single play may achieve at least two other kinds of unity: *formal* or analogical, and *final* or affective.[36]

Efforts to show formal unity in Dryden's play usually turn upon demonstrations of contrasts between the behavior and values of the characters in the comic action and those of the characters in the romantic heroic action. Whether we sum up the unifying analogy so discovered as "the vanity of all longing," or the "relation of love and honour to morality," or the dialectic interplay of "the fashionable and the idealized attitudes surrounding honor and 'propriety,' love and marriage, law and desire" is a matter of taste.[37] Clearly Dryden intends for us to perceive in the pure love of Leonidas and Palmyra something which contrasts with the proposed promiscuity of the four comic lovers, and in the duplicity of Argaleon and Polydamas something that parallels the contemplated duplicity of his comic characters. Yet his intention might have concerned final rather than formal unity, the affective rather than the analogical. As Rodes shows, the two kinds of scenes alternate with one another in a complex pattern that could only have been formed, not found.[38] The parts were to be "manag'd so regularly that the beauty of the whole be kept intire."[39] Just as the predictable shifts of key in a sonata allegro promise a return to the tonic and give shape to this temporal art, so does the alternation of a heroic world of romantic love with the mundane society of sexual passion promise a harmonious resolution, complete in time but no more reflective of reality than non-

---

[36] The Aristotelian terms "material," "efficient," "formal," and "final" are employed by Richard Levin in his discussion of dramatic unity in *The Multiple Plot in English Renaissance Drama* (Chicago, 1971), pp. 1–20.

[37] Myers, p. 58; King, p. 92; *Works*, 11: 478. See assertions of formal unity by Sutherland, p. 101, Rothstein, p. 148, and Hume, *Development*, p. 212; see also Okerlund's effort to subordinate the heroic to the comic plot in the interest of analogical unity; see as well *Works*, 11: 477, n. 81.

[38] *Works*, 11: 477–480.

[39] *An Essay of Dramatick Poesie*, in *Works*, 17: 49.

programmatic music or the artificial Restoration theater can be. The frivolity of the witty lovers lightens the potential disasters faced by Leonidas and Palmyra; the exalted honor and debased treachery of the characters of the heroic romantic plot leads us to perceive the promiscuity of the comic lovers as a temporary aberration viewed against the larger social scene. By the one we are assured of no tragedy in the other; by the other we are assured of the importance of the bonds of matrimonial love and law, even though characters talk of putting them aside. Were either plot missing, the other would become excessively melodramatic or lewdly suggestive. The beauty of the whole, its affective unity, lies in the amalgamation of the parts.[40]

The tastes that permitted Dryden to perfect the forms of his tragicomedies, these couplings of the romantic heroic and the comic, did not long endure. Bawdry became more popular, heroic plays less acceptable (or perhaps regarded as better suited to the operatic form). Humours comedy held its own while stories of fashionable Londoners engaged in witty sexual intrigue—the Etheregean pattern—found support. The last recorded performance of the complete *Marriage à la Mode* was on November 29, 1700, twenty-nine years after it appeared and seven months after the poet's death. Thereafter the romantic heroic and the comic plots were unyoked. The vitality of the comic sexual intrigue and particularly of Melantha proved itself in several eighteenth-century adaptations: an anonymous two-act version performed February 1 and 11, 1703; Colley Cibber's compilation (with the comic scenes of *Secret Love*), *The Comical Lovers; or, Marriage à la Mode*, beginning February 4, 1707, playing twenty-three times in the next fifteen years, and destined itself to be cut to three acts by John Philip Kemble for his wife's benefit night, May 23, 1796; and Henry Dell's afterpiece, *The Frenchified Lady Never in Paris*, per-

---

[40] For a valuable discussion of a different kind of affective unity, see Laura S. Brown, "The Divided Plot: Tragicomic Form in the Restoration," *ELH*, 47 (1980): 67–79, which came to hand after this work was in press. Brown emphasizes the difference between the serious plot of *Marriage à la Mode* and those of heroic drama, and the similarities between both plots and the Spanish *capa y espada* intrigue drama.

formed nineteen times over the seventeen years after its introduction on March 23, 1756.[41] But thereafter this play, "perhaps. . . the best of my comedies," as Dryden writes in his dedicatory epistle, became the sole property of playreaders who, in the twentieth century, have made it one of the most frequently reprinted Restoration comedies after those of Etherege, Wycherley, and Congreve.

I wish to thank my colleagues John B. Gabel and A. E. W. Maurer for advice, to acknowledge financial aid provided by Dean Michael W. Curran of the College of the Humanities, the Ohio State University, and to mention with great warmth the kind assistance of David M. Vieth, who supplied microfilm copies of nearly every text of *Marriage à la Mode* that I consulted.

MARK S. AUBURN

The Ohio State University

---

[41] This stage history emerges from *The London Stage, 1660–1800*, ed. William Van Lennep, Emmett L. Avery, Arthur H. Scouten, George Winchester Stone, Jr., Charles Beecher Hogan, 11 vols. (Carbondale, Ill., 1962–1968; parts one and two in revision by Arthur H. Scouten, Robert D. Hume, and Judith Milhous), *Index* compiled by Ben Ross Schneider, Jr. (Carbondale, 1979).

# MARRIAGE A LA MODE

*Quicquid sum ego, quamvis
Infra Lucili censum ingeniumque, tamen me
Cum magnis vixisse, invita fatebitur usque
Invidia, & fragili quaerens illidere dentem
Offendet solido.*

—Horat. Serm.

*Lucili*] C2; *Lucilli* Q1–4, om. epigraph
C1

---

*Quicquod . . . solido.*] Horace, *Satires*, II.i.74–79. "Such as I am—
inferior to Lucilius in rank, / Inferior in genius—even Envy will have to
admit/ That I too have lived with the great and, trying to sink/ Her tooth
into something soft, will grate on a rock" (Smith Palmer Bovie, *The Satires
and Epistles of Horace: A Modern English Verse Translation* [Chicago, 1959]).

# To the Right Honorable, the Earl of Rochester

My Lord,

I humbly dedicate to your lordship that poem of which you were pleased to appear an early patron before it was acted on the stage. I may yet go farther, with your permission, and say that it received amendment from your noble hands ere it was fit to be presented. You may 5 please likewise to remember with how much favor to the author and indulgence to the play you commended it to the view of His Majesty, then at Windsor, and by his approbation of it in writing, made way for its kind reception on the theater. In this dedication therefore I 10 may seem to imitate a custom of the ancients who offered to their gods the firstlings of the flock, which I think they called *ver sacrum* because they helped 'em to increase. I am sure if there be anything in this play wherein I have raised myself beyond the ordinary low- 15 ness of my comedies, I ought wholly to acknowledge it to the favor of being admitted into your lordship's conversation. And not only I, who pretend not to this way, but the best comic writers of our age will join with me to acknowledge that they have copied the gallantries of 20

5. ere] *normalized silently to this spelling throughout;* e're *Q1–2, C1–2;* e'er *Q3–4.*

0.1. *Rochester*] John Wilmot, second Earl of Rochester (1647–1680), dissolute and brilliant, court wit and gallant, artist and patron. Rochester was himself an excellent poet and a minor dramatist. Dryden's praise, though perhaps excessive to our tastes, is probably sincere. Within a year of the play's publication, however, Dryden and Rochester's relationship had cooled, and Rochester would never prove the patron or the political ally that Dryden probably hoped to make him.

8. *at Windsor*] *Works,* 11:487, notes that Charles II stayed at Windsor from May 27 to July 13 in 1671.

13. *ver sacrum*] a special offering presented from the first-born animals of spring.

courts, the delicacy of expression, and the decencies of
behavior from your lordship with more success than if
they had taken their models from the court of France.
But this, my lord, will be no wonder to the world, which
knows the excellency of your natural parts and those you       25
have acquired in a noble education. That which with
more reason I admire is that being so absolute a courtier
you have not forgot either the ties of friendship or the
practice of generosity. In my little experience of a court
(which I confess I desire not to improve) I have found in      30
it much of interest and more of detraction: few men
there have that assurance of a friend as not to be made
ridiculous by him when they are absent. There are a
middling sort of courtiers who become happy by their
want of wit; but they supply that want by an excess of        35
malice to those who have it. And there is no such perse-
cution as that of fools: they can never be considerable
enough to be talked of themselves, so that they are safe
only in their obscurity and grow mischievous to witty
men by the great diligence of their envy and by being         40
always present to represent and aggravate their faults. In
the meantime they are forced when they endeavor to be
pleasant to live on the offals of their wit whom they
decry, and either to quote it (which they do unwillingly)
or to pass it upon others for their own. These are the        45
men who make it their business to chase wit from the
knowledge of princes lest it should disgrace their ignorance. And this kind of malice your lordship has not so
much avoided as surmounted. But if by the excellent
temper of a royal master, always more ready to hear          50
good than ill; if by his inclination to love you; if by your
own merit and address; if by the charms of your conversation, the grace of your behavior, your knowledge of
greatness and habitude in courts you have been able to
preserve yourself with honor in the midst of so danger-       55
ous a course; yet at least the remembrance of those
hazards has inspired you with pity for other men who,

---

54. have] *C1–2;* having *Q1–4.*

43. *their wit whom*] the wit of those whom.

being of an inferior wit and quality to you, are yet perse-
cuted for being that in little which your lordship is in
great. For the quarrel of those people extends itself to   60
anything of sense and, if I may be so vain to own it
amongst the rest of the poets, has sometimes reached to
the very borders of it, even to me, so that if our general
good fortune had not raised up your lordship to defend
us, I know not whether anything had been more ridicu-   65
lous in court than writers. 'Tis to your lordship's favor
we generally owe our protection and patronage, and to
the nobleness of your nature, which will not suffer the
least shadow of your wit to be contemned in other men.
You have been often pleased not only to excuse my im-   70
perfections but to vindicate what was tolerable in my
writings from their censures. And what I never can
forget, you have not only been careful of my reputation
but of my fortune. You have been solicitous to supply my
neglect of myself and to overcome the fatal modesty of   75
poets, which submits them to perpetual wants rather
than to become importunate with those people who have
the liberality of kings in their disposing and who, dis-
honoring the bounty of their master, suffer such to be in
necessity who endeavor at least to please him and for   80
whose entertainment he has generously provided if the
fruits of his royal favor were not often stopped in other
hands. But your lordship has given me occasion not to
complain of courts whilst you are there. I have found the
effects of your mediation in all my concernments; and   85
they were so much the more noble in you because they
were wholly voluntary. I became your lordship's (if I may
venture on the similitude) as the world was made without
knowing him who made it, and brought only a passive
obedience to be your creature. This nobleness of yours I   90
think myself the rather obliged to own, because otherwise it must have been lost to all remembrance: for you

78. who,] *Q2–4, C1;* who *Q1, C2.*

---

60. *those people*] the "middling sort of courtiers" (1.34).
81. *entertainment*] sustenance.

are endued with that excellent quality of a frank nature,
to forget the good which you have done.

But, my lord, I ought to have considered that you are  95
as great a judge as you are a patron; and that in praising
you ill, I shall incur a higher note of ingratitude than
that I thought to have avoided. I stand in need of all
your accustomed goodness for the dedication of this play
which, though perhaps it be the best of my comedies, is 100
yet so faulty that I should have feared you for my critic if
I had not with some policy given you the trouble of being
my protector.Wit seems to have lodged itself more nobly
in this age than in any of the former; and people of my
mean condition are only writers because some of the 105
nobility, and your lordship in the first place, are above
the narrow praises which Poesie could give you. But let
those who love to see themselves exceeded encourage
your lordship in so dangerous a quality; for my own
part, I must confess that I have so much of self-interest 110
as to be content with reading some papers of your verses
without desiring you should proceed to a scene or play,
with the common prudence of those who are worsted in
a duel and declare they are satisfied when they are first
wounded. Your lordship has but another step to make, 115
and from the patron of wit, you may become its tyrant,
and oppress our little reputations with more ease than
you now protect them. But these, my lord, are designs
which I am sure you harbor not, any more than the
French king is contriving the conquest of the Swissers. 120
'Tis a barren triumph which is not worth your pains, and
would only rank him amongst your slaves who is already,

> My lord,
>
> Your lordship's
>
> Most obedient and most faithful servant, 125
>
> JOHN DRYDEN

100. which,    though    perhaps]    107. Poesie] *Q1, Q4, C1–2;* Posie
*Q2–4;* which though, perhaps, *Q1*    *Q2–3.*
*C1–2.*

# PROLOGUE

Lord, how reformed and quiet we are grown,
Since all our braves and all our wits are gone.
Fop-corner now is free from civil war:
White-wig and vizard make no longer jar.
France, and the fleet, have swept the town so clear,     5
That we can act in peace, and you can hear.
'Twas a sad sight, before they marched from home,  ⎤
To see our warriors, in red waistcoats, come        ⎬
With hair tucked up into our tiring-room.           ⎦
But 'twas more sad to hear their last adieu;      10
The women sobbed, and swore they would be true.
And so they were, as long as e'er they could:     ⎤
But powerful guinea cannot be withstood,        ⎬
And they were made of playhouse flesh and blood. ⎦
Fate did their friends for double use ordain:    ⎤ 15
In wars abroad they grinning honor gain,       ⎬
And mistresses, for all that stay, maintain.     ⎦
Now they are gone, 'tis dead vacation here,
For neither friends nor enemies appear.
Poor pensive punk now peeps ere plays begin,    20
Sees the bare bench, and dares not venture in,
But manages her last half-crown with care,
And trudges to the Mall, on foot, for air.
Our city friends so far will hardly come;

12. e'er] *normalized silently to this spelling throughout;* e're *Q1–4, C1–2.*

---

  2. *gone*] gone in preparation for the third Dutch war; see Introduction, p. xv.

  3. *Fop-corner*] a portion of the pit frequented by dandies.

  3. *civil war*] *Works*, 11:490, suggests an ironic pun on civil: "The fierce, primitive battle between the sexes as opposed to the impending international conflict."

  4. *White-wig*] Flaxen wigs were then fashionable for men.

  4. *vizard*] masks frequently worn by women, especially those of low repute, to the playhouse.

  20. *punk*] prostitute.

  23. *Mall*] a fashionable walk along St. James Park.

  24. *city*] the older, commercially oriented center of London; see III.i.113–181, Epilogue, l. 32.

They can take up with pleasures nearer home,        25
And see gay shows and gaudy scenes elsewhere:
For we presume they seldom come to hear.
But they have now ta'n up a glorious trade,
And cutting Moorcraft struts in masquerade.
There's all our hope, for we shall show today       30
A masquing ball to recommend our play:
Nay, to endear 'em more and let 'em see
We scorn to come behind in courtesy,
We'll follow the new mode which they begin,
And treat 'em with a room and couch within.       35
For that's one way, howe'er the play fall short,
T'oblige the town, the city, and the court.

29. Moorcraft]   *C2;*   Moorcraft,
*Q1–4; C1.*
35. room] *Q2–4;* room, *Q1, C1–2.*
37. T'oblige] *Q1, C1–2;* To oblige
*Q2–4.*

---

26. *elsewhere*] at the newly opened, elaborate theater in Dorset Gardens operated by the rival Duke's Company.
29. *cutting Moorcraft*] Moorcraft is the "swaggering blade" in Beaumont and Fletcher's *The Scornful Lady.*

# PERSONS REPRESENTED

## MEN

| | BY | |
|---|---|---|
| POLYDAMAS, usurper of Sicily | Mr. Wintershall | |
| LEONIDAS, the rightful prince, unknown | Mr. Kynaston | |
| ARGALEON, favorite to Polydamas | Mr. Lydall | 5 |
| HERMOGENES, foster-father to Leonidas | Mr. Cartwright | |
| EUBULUS, his friend and companion | Mr. Watson | |
| RHODOPHIL, captain of the guards | Mr. Mohun | |
| PALAMEDE, a courtier | Mr. Hart | |
| [STRATON, servant to Palamede's father] | | 10 |

## WOMEN

| | BY | |
|---|---|---|
| PALMYRA, daughter to the usurper | Mrs. Coxe | |
| AMALTHEA, sister to Argaleon | Mrs. James | |
| DORALICE, wife to Rhodophil | Mrs. Marshall | 15 |
| MELANTHA, an affected lady | Mrs. Bowtell | |
| PHILOTIS, woman to Melantha | Mrs. Reeve | |
| BELIZA, woman to Doralice | Mrs. Slade | |
| ARTEMIS, a court lady | Mrs. Uphill | |

Scene: *Sicily*

---

0.1. PERSONS REPRESENTED]
*Q1–4, C1;* Dramatis Personae *C2.*
2. BY] *Q1–4, C1; om. C2.*
3. POLYDAMAS] *Q1–2, C1–2, normalized silently to this spelling through-*
out; Polydamus *Q3–4.*
18. BELIZA] *C2, normalized silently to this spelling throughout;* Belisa *Q1–4, C1.*

# Marriage à la Mode

## ACT I

*Scene: Walks near the court.*
*Enter* Doralice *and* Beliza.

DORALICE.

Beliza, bring the lute into this arbor, the walks are
empty: I would try the song the princess Amalthea bade
me learn.

*They go in, and sing.*

1

    Why should a foolish marriage vow
      Which long ago was made,             5
    Oblige us to each other now
      When passion is decayed?
    We loved, and we loved, as long as we could,
      Till our love was loved out in us both.
    But our marriage is dead, when the pleasure is fled: 10
      'Twas pleasure first made it an oath.

2

    If I have pleasures for a friend,
      And farther love in store,
    What wrong has he whose joys did end,
      And who could give no more?         15
    'Tis a madness that he should be jealous of me,
      Or that I should bar him of another;

16. 'Tis . . . me] *C1;* 'Tis . . . he/
Should . . . me *Q1–4, C2.*
17. another;] *this edn.;* another?
*Q1, C1–2;* another: *Q2–4.*

> For all we can gain is to give ourselves pain,
> When neither can hinder the other.

*Enter* Palamede, *in riding habit, and hears the song.*
*Re-enter* Doralice *and* Beliza.

BELIZA.

Madam, a stranger.      20

DORALICE.

I did not think to have had witnesses of my bad singing.

PALAMEDE.

If I have erred, madam, I hope you'll pardon the curiosity of a stranger, for I may well call myself so after five
years' absence from the court. But you have freed me
from one error.      25

DORALICE.

What's that, I beseech you?

PALAMEDE.

I thought good voices and ill faces had been inseparable,
and that to be fair and sing well had been only the privi-
lege of angels.

DORALICE.

And how many more of these fine things can you say to   30
me?

PALAMEDE.

Very few, madam, for if I should continue to see you
some hours longer, you look so killingly that I should be
mute with wonder.

DORALICE.

This will not give you the reputation of a wit with me.   35
You travelling *monsieurs* live upon the stock you have got
abroad for the first day or two; to repeat with a good
memory and apply with a good grace is all your wit. And
commonly your gullets are sewed up like cormorants:
when you have regorged what you have taken in, you are   40
the leanest things in nature.

18. For . . . pain] *C1*; For . . . gain/     23. myself so] *Q1–2, Q4, C1–2;* so
Is . . . pain *Q1–4, C2.*                      *Q3.*

39. *gullets . . . cormorants*] Seabirds whose throats were tied shut with
a leather thong were used for fishing.

PALAMEDE.

Then, madam, I think you had best make that use of me;
let me wait on you for two or three days together, and
you shall hear all I have learnt of extraordinary in other
countries. And one thing which I never saw till I came 45
home, that is a lady of a better voice, better face, and
better wit than any I have seen abroad. And, after this, if
I should not declare myself most passionately in love
with you, I should have less wit than yet you think I have.

DORALICE.

A very plain and pithy declaration. I see, sir, you have 50
been travelling in Spain or Italy or some of the hot
countries where men come to the point immediately. But
are you sure these are not words of course? For I would
not give my poor heart an occasion of complaint against
me, that I engaged it too rashly and then could not bring 55
it off.

PALAMEDE.

Your heart may trust itself with me safely. I shall use it
very civilly while it stays, and never turn it away without
fair warning to provide for itself.

DORALICE.

First, then, I do receive your passion with as little con- 60
sideration on my part as ever you gave it me on yours.
And now see what a miserable wretch you have made
yourself.

PALAMEDE.

Who, I miserable? Thank you for that. Give me love
enough, and life enough, and I defy fortune. 65

DORALICE.

Know then, thou man of vain imagination, know to thy
utter confusion that I am virtuous.

PALAMEDE.

Such another word and I give up the ghost.

DORALICE.

Then, to strike you quite dead, know that I am married,
too. 70

---

53. *of course*] of custom, of fashion.

PALAMEDE.

Art thou married? O thou damnable virtuous woman!

DORALICE.

Yes, married to a gentleman, young, handsome, rich, valiant, and with all the good qualities that will make you despair and hang yourself.

PALAMEDE.

Well, in spite of all that I'll love you. Fortune has cut us   75
out for one another, for I am to be married within these three days: married past redemption to a young, fair, rich, and virtuous lady. And it shall go hard, but I will love my wife as little as I perceive you do your husband.

DORALICE.

Remember, I invade no propriety. My servant you are   80
only till you are married.

PALAMEDE.

In the meantime, you are to forget you have a husband.

DORALICE.

And you, that you are to have a wife.

BELIZA (aside to her lady).

O madam, my lord's just at the end of the walks, and if
you make not haste will discover you.                    85

DORALICE.

Some other time, new servant, we'll talk further of the premises; in the meanwhile, break not my first commandment: that is, not to follow me.

PALAMEDE.

But where, then, shall I find you again?

DORALICE.

At court. Yours for two days, sir.                        90

PALAMEDE.

And nights, I beseech you, madam.

                              Exeunt Doralice and Beliza.

Well, I'll say that for thee, thou art a very dextrous executioner; thou has done my business at one stroke. Yet I

---

71. married?] this edn.; married;   C1–2.
Q1–4, C1–2.                          91.1. Exeunt] this edn.; Exit Q1–4,
71. woman!] Q2–4; woman? Q1,   C1–2.
C1–2.

---

80. propriety] property.
80. servant] male lover (in the chivalric sense).

must marry another—and yet I must love this. And if it
lead me into some little inconveniencies, as jealousies  95
and duels and death and so forth, yet while sweet love is
in the case, fortune do thy worst and avaunt mortality.

*Enter* Rhodophil, *who seems speaking to one within.*

RHODOPHIL.
Leave 'em with my lieutenant while I fetch new orders
from the king. (*Sees* Palamede.)   How? Palamede!

PALAMEDE.
Rhodophil!                                              100

RHODOPHIL.
Who thought to have seen you in Sicily?

PALAMEDE.
Who thought to have found the court so far from Syracuse?

RHODOPHIL.
The king best knows the reason of the progress. But
answer me, I beseech you, what brought you home from  105
travel?

PALAMEDE.
The commands of an old rich father.

RHODOPHIL.
And the hopes of burying him?

PALAMEDE.
Both together, as you see, have prevailed on my good
nature. In few words, my old man has already married  110
me, for he has agreed with another old man as rich and
as covetous as himself; the articles are drawn, and I have
given my consent, for fear of being disinherited, and yet
know not what kind of woman I am to marry.

RHODOPHIL.
Sure your father intends you some very ugly wife, and  115
has a mind to keep you in ignorance till you have shot
the gulf.

97.1. Rhodophil] *C1–2, normalized*      Rodophil *Q1–4.*
*silently to this spelling throughout;*

_____

95. *as*] such as.
    116–117. *have shot the gulf*] are past the point of no return; but see
*OED,* gulf, II.2.b.

PALAMEDE.

I know not that, but obey I will and must.

RHODOPHIL.

Then I cannot choose but grieve for all the good girls
and courtesans of France and Italy. They have lost the 120
most kind-hearted, doting, prodigal, humble servant in
Europe.

PALAMEDE.

All I could do in these three years I stayed behind you
was to comfort the poor creatures for the loss of you. But
what's the reason that in all this time a friend could never 125
hear from you?

RHODOPHIL.

Alas, dear Palamede, I have had no joy to write nor
indeed to do anything in the world to please me. The
greatest misfortune imaginable is fallen upon me.

PALAMEDE.

Prithee, what's the matter?                                      130

RHODOPHIL.

In one word, I am married, wretchedly married, and
have been above these two years. Yes, faith, the devil has
had power over me in spite of my vows and resolutions
to the contrary.

PALAMEDE.

I find you have sold yourself for filthy lucre: she's old or 135
ill-conditioned.

RHODOPHIL.

No, none of these. I'm sure she's young; and, for her
humor, she laughs, sings, and dances eternally; and,
which is more, we never quarrel about it, for I do the
same.                                                           140

PALAMEDE.

You're very unfortunate indeed. Then the case is plain:
she's not handsome.

RHODOPHIL.

A great beauty, too, as people say.

---

119. *good girls*] wanton wenches (*A Dictionary of Slang,* Partridge).
136. *ill-conditioned*] of mean social status.
138. *humor*] disposition.

PALAMEDE.

As people say? Why, you should know that best yourself.

RHODOPHIL.

Ask those who have smelled to a strong perfume two 145
years together what's the scent.

PALAMEDE.

But here are good qualities enough for one woman.

RHODOPHIL.

Ay, too many, Palamede; if I could put 'em into three or
four women, I should be content.

PALAMEDE.

O, now I have found it: you dislike her for no other 150
reason but because she's your wife.

RHODOPHIL.

And is not that enough? All that I know of her perfections now is only by memory. I remember, indeed, that
about two years ago I loved her passionately; but those
golden days are gone, Palamede. Yet I loved her a whole 155
half year, double the natural term of any mistress, and
think in my conscience I could have held out another
quarter. But then the world began to laugh at me, and a
certain shame of being out of fashion seized me. At last
we arrived at that point that there was nothing left in us 160
to make us new to one another. Yet still I set a good face
upon the matter and am infinite fond of her before
company; but, when we are alone, we walk like lions in a
room, she one way and I another, and we lie with our
backs to each other so far distant as if the fashion of 165
great beds was only invented to keep husband and wife
sufficiently asunder.

PALAMEDE.

The truth is, your disease is very desperate; but though
you cannot be cured, you may be patched up a little. You
must get you a mistress, Rhodophil. That, indeed, is liv- 170
ing upon cordials: but as fast as one fails you must supply

144. that best] *Q1–4, C2;* best that
*C1.*

---

166. *great beds*] double beds, a recent fashion (B-B, p. 289).
171. *cordials*] medicinal beverages or foods.

it with another. You're like a gamester who has lost his
estate: yet in doing that, you have learned the advantages of play and can arrive to live upon't.

RHODOPHIL.

Truth is, I have been thinking on't, and have just re- 175
solved to take your counsel. And, faith, considering the
damned disadvantages of a married man, I have provided well enough for a poor humble sinner that is not
ambitious of great matters.

PALAMEDE.

What is she, for a woman?                         180

RHODOPHIL.

One of the stars of Syracuse, I assure you: young
enough, fair enough, and but for one quality, just such a
woman as I would wish.

PALAMEDE.

O friend, this is not an age to be critical in beauty. When
we had good store of handsome women and but few 185
chapmen, you might have been more curious in your
choice; but now the price is enhanced upon us, and all
mankind set up for mistresses, so that poor little creatures without beauty, birth, or breeding but only impudence go off at unreasonable rates; and a man in these 190
hard times snaps at 'em as he does at broad-gold, never
examines the weight but takes light or heavy as he can
get it.

RHODOPHIL.

But my mistress has one fault that's almost unpardon-
able; for, being a town-lady without any relation to the 195
court, yet she thinks herself undone if she be not seen
there three or four times a day with the princess Amal-

---

196–197. seen there] *Q1–4, C2;*
seen *C1.*

186. *chapmen*] purchasers, customers (*OED*).
186. *curious*] precisely accurate (*OED*).
191. *broad-gold*] twenty-shilling pieces ("Jacobus" and "Carolus")
minted in the reigns of James I and Charles I, broader and thinner than
the milled guineas minted after 1663. Broad-pieces had smooth edges and
hence could be easily shaved or clipped.
195. *town-lady*] lady of the town rather than the city, the country, or
the court; not necessarily pejorative; cf. III.i.113–181.

thea. And for the king, she haunts and watches him so
narrowly in a morning that she prevents even the chem-
ists who beset his chamber to turn their mercury into his 200
gold.

PALAMEDE.

Yet hitherto, methinks, you are no very unhappy man.

RHODOPHIL.

With all this, she's the greatest gossip in nature; for,
besides the court, she's the most eternal visiter of the
town, and yet manages her time so well that she seems 205
ubiquitary. For my part, I can compare her to nothing
but the sun: for like him she takes no rest, nor ever
sets in one place but to rise in another.

PALAMEDE.

I confess she had need be handsome with these qualities.

RHODOPHIL.

No lady can be so curious of a new fashion as she is of a 210
new French word; she's the very mint of the nation, and
as fast as any bullion comes out of France, coins it immediately into our language.

PALAMEDE.

And her name is—

RHODOPHIL.

No naming; that's not like a cavalier. Find her if you can 215
by my description and I am not so ill a painter that I
need write the name beneath the picture.

PALAMEDE.

Well then, how far have you proceeded in your love?

RHODOPHIL.

'Tis yet in the bud, and what fruit it may bear I cannot
tell, for this insufferable humor of haunting the court is 220
so predominant that she has hitherto broken all her assignations with me for fear of missing her visits there.

208. another] *Q1–3, C1–2;* an
other *Q4.*
215. Find] *begins new paragraph*
*Q1–4, C1–2.*

---

199. *prevents*] precedes (*OED*).
200. *mercury*] used in the treatment of venereal diseases.
206. *ubiquitary*] ubiquitous (*OED*).

PALAMEDE.

That's the hardest part of your adventure. But, for
aught I see, fortune has used us both alike: I have a
strange kind of mistress too in court, besides her I am to 225
marry.

RHODOPHIL.

You have made haste to be in love then, for if I am not
mistaken you are but this day arrived.

PALAMEDE.

That's all one. I have seen the lady already who has
charmed me, seen her in these walks, courted her, and 230
received for the first time an answer that does not put me
into despair.

        *To them,* Argaleon, Amalthea, Artemis.

I'll tell you at more leisure my adventures. The walks fill
apace, I see. Stay, is not that the young lord Argaleon,
the king's favorite?                               235

RHODOPHIL.

Yes, and as proud as ever, as ambitious, and as revenge-
ful.

PALAMEDE.

How keeps he the king's favor with these qualities?

RHODOPHIL.

Argaleon's father helped him to the crown. Besides, he
gilds over all his vices to the king, and standing in the 240
dark to him, sees all his inclinations, interests, and humors, which he so times and soothes that, in effect, he
reigns.

PALAMEDE.

His sister Amalthea, who I guess stands by him, seems
not to be of his temper.                            245

RHODOPHIL.

O, she's all goodness and generosity.

ARGALEON.

Rhodophil, the king expects you earnestly.

---

227. haste] *Q1–3, C1–2;* hast *Q4.*    240. vices] *Q1–4, C2;* voices *C1.*
236. and as proud] *Q1–3, C1–2;* as   247. king] *Q1–2, Q4, C1–2;* kings
proud *Q4.*                                   *Q3.*

    247. *expects*] awaits (*OED*).

RHODOPHIL.

    'Tis done, my lord, what he commanded. I only waited
    his return from hunting. Shall I attend your lordship to
    him?                                                        250

ARGALEON.

    No. I go first another way.                *Exit hastily.*

PALAMEDE.

    He seems in haste and discomposed.

AMALTHEA (*to* Rhodophil *after a short whisper*).

    Your friend? Then he must needs be of much merit.

RHODOPHIL.

    When he has kissed the king's hand, I know he'll beg the
    honor to kiss yours. Come, Palamede.                 255

        *Exeunt* Rhodophil *and* Palamede *bowing to* Amalthea.

ARTEMIS.

    Madam, you tell me most surprising news.

AMALTHEA.

    The fear of it, you see,
    Has discomposed my brother; but to me
    All that can bring my country good is welcome.

ARTEMIS.

    It seems incredible that this old king,                  260
    Whom all the world thought childless,
    Should come to search the farthest parts of Sicily
    In hope to find an heir.

AMALTHEA.

    To lessen your astonishment, I will
    Unfold some private passages of state                    265
    Of which you yet are ignorant. Know first
    That this Polydamas, who reigns, unjustly
    Gained the crown.

ARTEMIS.

    Somewhat of this I have confus'dly heard.

AMALTHEA.

    I'll tell you all in brief. Theagenes,                   270

---

252. S.P. PALAMEDE. He ... dis-
composed.] *Q1, C1–2; om. Q2–4.*

---

265. *passages*] transactions or proceedings (*OED*, III.13).

    Our last great king,
    Had by his queen one only son, an infant
    Of three years old, called after him Theagenes:
    The general, this Polydamas, then married;
    The public feasts for which were scarcely past       275
    When a rebellion in the heart of Sicily
    Called out the king to arms.
ARTEMIS.                         Polydamas
    Had then a just excuse to stay behind.
AMALTHEA.
    His temper was too warlike to accept it.
    He left his bride and the new joys of marriage      280
    And followed to the field. In short they fought,
    The rebels were o'ercome; but in the fight
    The too bold king received a mortal wound.
    When he perceived his end approaching near,
    He called the general, to whose care he left      285
    His widow queen and orphan son, then died.
ARTEMIS.
    Then false Polydamas betrayed his trust?
AMALTHEA.
    He did; and with my father's help, for which
    Heav'n pardon him, so gained the soldiers' hearts
    That in few days he was saluted king.      290
    And when his crimes had impudence enough
    To bear the eye of day,
    He marched his army back to Syracuse.
    But see how heav'n can punish wicked men
    In granting their desires: the news was brought him     295
    That day he was to enter it that Eubulus,
    Whom his dead master had left governor,
    Was fled and with him bore away the queen
    And royal orphan. But what more amazed him,
    His wife, now big with child and much detesting     300
    Her husband's practices, had willingly
    Accompanied their flight.
ARTEMIS.
    How I admire her virtue!
AMALTHEA.                  What became
    Of her and them since that was never known.

Only, some few days since a famous robber              305
Was taken with some jewels of vast price
Which, when they were delivered to the king,
He knew had been his wife's; with these a letter,
Much torn and sullied, but which yet he knew
To be her writing.

ARTEMIS.                    Sure from hence he learned     310
He had a son.

AMALTHEA.        It was not left so plain.
The paper only said she died in childbed.
But when it should have mentioned son or daughter,
Just there it was torn off.

ARTEMIS.                        Madam, the king.

*To them,* Polydamas, Argaleon, *Guard, and Attendants.*

ARGALEON.

The robber, though thrice racked, confessed no more 315
But that he took those jewels near this place.

POLYDAMAS.

But yet the circumstances strongly argue
That those for whom I search are not far off.

ARGALEON.

I cannot easily believe it.

ARTEMIS (*aside*).                    No,
You would not have it so.                               320

POLYDAMAS.

Those I employed have, in the neighboring hamlet
Amongst the fishers' cabins, made discovery
Of some young persons whose uncommon beauty
And graceful carriage make it seem suspicious
They are not what they seem. I therefore sent        325
The captain of my guards this morning early
With orders to secure and bring 'em to me.

*Enter* Rhodophil *and* Palamede.

O, here he is. Have you performed my will?

---

314.1. *Guard*] Q1–4, C1–2, Sutherland, B-B; *Guards Works.*

314.1. *Guard*] a troop of guards.

RHODOPHIL.

    Sir, those whom you commanded me to bring
    Are waiting in the walks.

POLYDAMAS.

                             Conduct 'em hither.        330

RHODOPHIL.

    First give me leave
    To beg your notice of this gentleman.

POLYDAMAS.

    He seems to merit it. His name and quality?

RHODOPHIL.

    Palamede, son to Lord Cleodemus of Palermo,
    And new returned from travel.

    Palamede *approaches, and kneels to kiss the king's hand.*

POLYDAMAS.                   You're welcome.        335
    I knew your father well; he was both brave
    And honest; we two once were fellow soldiers
    In the last civil wars.

PALAMEDE.

    I bring the same unquestioned honesty
    And zeal to serve your majesty; the courage    340
    You were pleased to praise in him,
    Your royal prudence and your people's love
    Will never give me leave to try like him
    In civil wars; I hope it may in foreign.

POLYDAMAS.

    Attend the court, and it shall be my care    345
    To find out some employment worthy you.
    Go, Rhodophil, and bring in those without.

                        *Exeunt* Rhodophil *and* Palamede.

Rhodophil *returns immediately, and with him enter* Hermogenes,
Leonidas, *and* Palmyra.

    Behold two miracles!

---

334. son to] *Q1, C1–2;* son to the
*Q2–4.*
335. You're] *Q1–4, C1;* You are
*C2.*

342. and  your] *Q1–2, Q4, C1–2;*
and you *Q3.*
348. miracles!] *Q1, C1–2;* miracles
*Q2–4.*

*Looking earnestly on* Leonidas *and* Palmyra.

Of different sexes but of equal form.
So matchless both that my divided soul                    350
Can scarcely ask the gods a son or daughter
For fear of losing one. If from your hands,
You powers, I shall this day receive a daughter,
Argaleon, she is yours; but if a son,
Then Amalthea's love shall make him happy.                    355

ARGALEON.

Grant, heav'n, this admirable nymph may prove
That issue which he seeks.

AMALTHEA.

Venus Urania, if thou art a goddess,
Grant that sweet youth may prove the prince of Sicily.

POLYDAMAS (*to* Hermogenes).

Tell me, old man, and tell me true, from whence                    360
Had you that youth and maid?

HERMOGENES.                    From whence you had
Your scepter, sir: I had 'em from the gods.

POLYDAMAS.

The gods then have not such another gift.
Say who their parents were.

HERMOGENES.                    My wife and I.

ARGALEON.

It is not likely                    365
A virgin of so excellent a beauty
Should come from such a stock.

AMALTHEA.

Much less that such a youth, so sweet, so graceful,
Should be produced from peasants.

HERMOGENES.

Why, nature is the same in villages                    370

353. daughter,] *Q1*, *C1–2*; 365–366. It . . . likely/ A virgin
daughter. *Q2–4*.                    . . . beauty] *Works; one line Q1–4,*
354. but] *Q1–4, C2;* but but *C1*.                    *C1–2, Sutherland, B-B.*

358. *Venus Urania*] daughter of Uranus, who exercises dominion
over beauty and generation.

And much more fit to form a noble issue
Where it is least corrupted.

POLYDAMAS.

He talks too like a man that knew the world
To have been long a peasant. But the rack
Will teach him other language. Hence with him.     375

*As the Guard are carrying him away, his peruke falls off.*

Sure I have seen that face before. Hermogenes!
'Tis he, 'tis he who fled away with Eubulus
And with my dear Eudoxia.

HERMOGENES.

Yes, sir, I am Hermogenes.
And if to have been loyal be a crime,               380
I stand prepared to suffer.

POLYDAMAS.

If thou wouldst live, speak quickly:
What is become of my Eudoxia?
Where is the queen and young Theagenes?
Where Eubulus? and which of these is mine?          385

*Pointing to* Leonidas *and* Palmyra.

HERMOGENES.

Eudoxia is dead, so is the queen,
The infant king her son, and Eubulus.

POLYDAMAS.

Traitor, 'tis false: produce 'em or—

HERMOGENES.              Once more
I tell you, they are dead; but leave to threaten,
For you shall know no further.                      390

POLYDAMAS.

Then prove indulgent to my hopes and be
My friend forever. Tell me, good Hermogenes,
Whose son is that brave youth?

---

375.1. *Guard*] *Q1, C1–2, Suther-*    *C1–2, Sutherland, B-B;* Eudocia
*land, B-B;* Guards *Q2–4, Works.*      *Works* (*see Introduction to this edn., p.*
378, 383, 386. Eudoxia] *Q1–4,*        *xiv*).

    389. *leave*] cease.

HERMOGENES.                    Sir, he is yours.
POLYDAMAS.
    Fool that I am, thou see'st that so I wish it
    And so thou flatter'st me.
HERMOGENES.                    By all that's holy.          395
POLYDAMAS.
    Again. Thou canst not swear too deeply.
    Yet hold, I will believe thee—yet I doubt.
HERMOGENES.
    You need not, sir.
ARGALEON.
    Believe him not; he sees you credulous
    And would impose his own base issue on you        400
    And fix it to your crown.
AMALTHEA.
    Behold his goodly shape and feature, sir;
    Methinks he much resembles you.
ARGALEON.
    I say, if you have any issue here,
    It must be that fair creature;                    405
    By all my hopes I think so.
AMALTHEA.
    Yes, brother, I believe you by your hopes,
    For they are all for her.
POLYDAMAS.                    Call the youth nearer.
HERMOGENES.
    Leonidas, the king would speak with you.
POLYDAMAS.
    Come near, and be not dazzled with the splendor    410
    And greatness of a court.
LEONIDAS.
    I need not this encouragement.
    I can fear nothing but the gods.
    And for this glory, after I have seen
    The canopy of state spread wide above             415
    In the abyss of heaven, the court of stars,

401. to] *Q1–3, C1–2;* on *Q4.*
410. with the] *Q1–3, C1–2;* with
*Q4.*

– 27 –

The blushing morning, and the rising sun,
What greater can I see?

POLYDAMAS (*embracing him*).

This speaks thee born a prince; thou art thyself
That rising sun and shalt not see on earth                    420
A brighter than thyself. —All of you witness
That for my son I here receive this youth,
This brave, this—but I must not praise him further
Because he now is mine.

LEONIDAS (*kneeling*).

I wonnot, sir, believe                                        425
That I am made your sport;
For I find nothing in myself but what
Is much above a scorn; I dare give credit
To whatsoe'er a king, like you, can tell me.
Either I am or will deserve to be your son.                   430

ARGALEON.

I yet maintain it is impossible
That this young man should be yours; for if he were,
Why should Hermogenes so long conceal him
When he might gain so much by his discovery?

HERMOGENES (*to the king*).

I stayed a while to make him worthy, sir, of you.             435
But in that time I found
Somewhat within him which so moved my love
I never could resolve to part with him.

LEONIDAS (*to* Argaleon).

You ask too many questions and are
Too saucy for a subject.                                      440

ARGALEON.

You rather overact your part and are
Too soon a prince.

LEONIDAS.                    Too soon you'll find me one.

---

419. thee] *Q1–2, Q4, C1–2;* the *Q3*.
420. sun] *Q1–2, C1–2;* son *Q3–4.*
423. further] *Q1–4, C2;* farther *C1.*
425–426. believe/  That]  *Q1–4,*

*C1–2, Sutherland, Works;* Believe
that *B-B.*
429. whatsoe'er] *Q3–4, C1–2;* whatsoe'r *Q1–2.*

POLYDAMAS.

    Enough, Argaleon,
    I have declared him mine; and you, Leonidas,
    Live well with him I love.           445

ARGALEON.

    Sir, if he be your son, I may have leave
    To think your queen had twins. Look on this virgin:
    Hermogenes would enviously deprive you
    Of half your treasure.

HERMOGENES.         Sir, she is my daughter.

    I could, perhaps, thus aided by this lord     450
    Prefer her to be yours; but truth forbid
    I should procure her greatness by a lie.

POLYDAMAS.

    Come hither, beauteous maid. Are you not sorry
    Your father will not let you pass for mine?

PALMYRA.

    I am content to be what heav'n has made me.     455

POLYDAMAS.

    Could you not wish yourself a princess then?

PALMYRA.

    Not to be sister to Leonidas.

POLYDAMAS.

    Why, my sweet maid?         Indeed I cannot tell;
    But I could be content to be his handmaid.

ARGALEON *(aside)*.

    I wish I had not seen her.         460

PALMYRA *(to* Leonidas).

    I must weep for your good fortune;
    Pray pardon me, indeed I cannot help it.
    Leonidas (alas, I had forgot,
    Now I must call you prince), but must I leave you?

LEONIDAS *(aside)*.

    I dare not speak to her; for if I should,     465

---

451. forbid] *Q1–3, C1–2;* forbid.   *C1–2; displaced two ems to right as if*
*Q4.*                                    *S.P. Q1.*
463. Leonidas] *left justified Q2–4,*

I must weep too.

POLYDAMAS.

    No, you shall live at court, sweet innocence,
    And see him there. Hermogenes,
    Though you intended not to make me happy,
    Yet you shall be rewarded for th'event.          470
    Come, my Leonidas, let's thank the gods,
    Thou for a father, I for such a son.

                *Exeunt all but* Leonidas *and* Palmyra.

LEONIDAS.

    My dear Palmyra, many eyes observe me,
    And I have thoughts so tender that I cannot
    In public speak 'em to you. Some hours hence      475
    I shall shake off these crowds of fawning courtiers,
    And then—

                            *Exit* Leonidas.

PALMYRA.

    Fly swift, you hours, you measure time for me in vain
    Till you bring back Leonidas again.
    Be shorter now, and to redeem that wrong,        480
    When he and I are met, be twice as long.

                                *Exit.*

476. courtiers,] *Q1, C1–2;* courtiers. *Q2–4.*

# ACT II

[*Enter*] Melantha *and* Philotis.

PHILOTIS.

Count Rhodophil's a fine gentleman indeed, madam,
and I think deserves your affection.

MELANTHA.

Let me die but he's a fine man; he sings and dances *en
Français* and writes *billets-doux* to a miracle.

PHILOTIS.

And those are no small talents to a lady that understands     5
and values the French *air* as your ladyship does.

MELANTHA.

How charming is the French *air!* and what an *étourdi bête*
is one of our untravelled islanders! when he would make
his court to me, let me die but he is just Æsop's ass that
would imitate the courtly French in his addresses, but     10
instead of those, comes pawing upon me and doing all
things so *maladroitly*.

PHILOTIS.

'Tis great pity Rhodophil's a married man, that you may
not have an honorable *intrigue* with him.

MELANTHA.

*Intrigue*, Philotis! That's an old phrase. I have laid that     15
word by: *amour* sounds better. But thou art heir to all my
cast words, as thou art to my old wardrobe. O Count
Rhodophil! Ah *mon cher!* I could live and die with him.

*Enter* Palamede *and a Servant.*

SERVANT.

Sir, this is my lady.

9. he] *Q1–4, C2;* we *C1.*
14, 15. *intrigue*] *this edn.;* intrigue
*Q1–4, C1–2.*

---

6,7. *air*] "Air," in the sense of appearance or demeanor, arrived in
English from the French only about 1600 (*OED*), so the two ladies may
give it a French pronunciation.
7. *étourdi bête*] thoughtless beast.
9. *Æsop's ass*] In the fable, the ass who imitates a lapdog.

PALAMEDE.

Then this is she that is to be divine, and nymph, and      20
goddess, and with whom I am to be desperately in love.

*Bows to her, delivering a letter.*

This letter, madam, which I present you from your
father, has given me both the happy opportunity, and
the boldness, to kiss the fairest hands in Sicily.

MELANTHA.

Came you lately from Palermo, sir?                          25

PALAMEDE.

But yesterday, madam.

MELANTHA *(reading the letter).*

"Daughter, receive the bearer of this letter as a gentleman whom I have chosen to make you happy." (O
Venus, a new servant sent me! and let me die but he has
the air of a gallant *homme.)* "His father is the rich lord   30
Cleodemus, our neighbor. I suppose you'll find nothing
disagreeable in his person or his converse, both which he
has improved by travel. The treaty is already concluded,
and I shall be in town within these three days, so that
you have nothing to do but to obey your careful fa-        35
ther." (*To* Palamede.) Sir, my father, for whom I
have a blind obedience, has commanded me to receive
your passionate addresses; but you must also give me
leave to avow that I cannot merit 'em from so accom-
plished a cavalier.                                         40

PALAMEDE.

I want many things, madam, to render me accom-
plished; and the first and greatest of 'em is your favor.

MELANTHA [*aside to* Philotis].

Let me die, Philotis, but this is extremely French; but yet,
Count Rhodophil. —A gentleman, sir, that understands
the *grand monde* so well, who has haunted the best *con-*   45

45–47. *conversations . . . voyaged . . .*        aged, graces *Q1–4, C1–2.*
*grâces*] *this edn.;* conversations, voy-

32. *converse*] "familiar interchange of thoughts; discourse; talk; =
conversation" (OED).

45–47. *conversations. . . . voyaged . . . grâces*] That Melantha pro-
nounces these words (spelled as English in Qq, Cc) with a French accent is
strongly suggested by Palamede's following line (Sutherland, p. 142).

*versations,* and who (in short) has *voyaged,* may pretend to
the good *grâces* of any lady.

PALAMEDE *(aside).*

Hey day! *Grande monde! conversation! voyaged!* and good
*grâces!* I find my mistress is one of those that run mad in
new French words.                                                    50

MELANTHA.

I suppose, sir, you have made the *tour* of France, and
having seen all that's fine there, will make a considerable
reformation in the rudeness of our court: for, let me die,
but an unfashioned, untravelled, mere Sicilian is a *bête*
and has nothing in the world of an *honnête homme.*   55

PALAMEDE.

I must confess, madam, that—

MELANTHA.

And what new *minuets* have you brought over with you?
Their *minuets* are to a miracle! And our Sicilian *jigs* are so
dull and *fade* to 'em!

PALAMEDE.

For *minuets,* madam—                                                60

MELANTHA.

And what new plays are there in vogue? And who
danced best in the last grand ballet? Come, sweet servant, you shall tell me all.

PALAMEDE *(aside).*

Tell her all? why, she asks all and will hear nothing. —To
answer in order, madam, to your demands—                             65

MELANTHA.

I am thinking what a happy couple we shall be! For you
shall keep up your correspondence abroad, and everything that's new writ in France and fine, I mean all that's
delicate and *bien tourné,* we will have first.

---

47. any] *Q1–4, C1;* a *C2.*          58. *jigs] Q1–4;* jigs *C1–2, Works.*
57. you?] *C1, Works;* you! *Q1–4,*   59. *fade] Works;* fad *Q1;* sad *Q2–4,*
*C2.*                                  *C1–2, Sutherland, B-B.*

52. *fine]* Perhaps Melantha says "*fin*" (refined).
54. *bête]* beast.
55. *honnête homme]* literally, "honest man"; figuratively, well-bred
gentleman.
59. *fade]* insipid, tasteless.      68. *fine]* See above, II.52n.
69. *bien tourné]* well fashioned, well expressed.

PALAMEDE.

But, madam, our fortune—                                          70

MELANTHA.

I understand you, sir; you'll leave that to me. For the
*ménage* of a family, I know it better than any lady in
Sicily.

PALAMEDE.

Alas, madam, we—

MELANTHA.

Then, we will never make visits together nor see a play,    75
but always apart. You shall be every day at the king's *levé*,
and I at the queen's; and we will never meet but in the
drawing-room.

PHILOTIS.

Madam, the new prince is just passed by the end of the
walk.                                                            80

MELANTHA.

The new prince, say'st thou? Adieu, dear servant; I have
not made my court to him these two long hours. O, 'tis
the sweetest prince! So *obligeant, charmant, ravissant,*
that— Well, I'll make haste to kiss his hands, and then
make half a score visits more, and be with you again in a    85
twinkling.                               *Exit, running with* Philotis.

PALAMEDE (*solus*).

Now heaven, of thy mercy, bless me from this tongue; it
may keep the field against a whole army of lawyers, and
that in their own language, French gibberish. 'Tis true,
in the daytime 'tis tolerable, when a man has field-room    90
to run from it; but to be shut up in a bed with her, like

---

72. *ménage*] Sutherland, B-B; men-
nage *Q1–2, C1–2, Works;* mannage
*Q3–4.*
79. by the] *Q1–3, C1–2;* the *Q4.*

83. *obligeant, charmant, ravissant*]
Sutherland, B-B, Works; obligeant,
charmant, ravissant *Q1–4, C1–2.*
88. the] *Q1–3, C1–2;* thee *Q4.*

---

77. *queen's*] Melantha's imaginary world includes a queen, although
Polydamas is an unmarried widower.

82. *these two long hours*] "The prince's presence has been known for
only two hours, but Melantha has not yet met him" (*Works,* 11:497).

89. *French gibberish*] legal French, the compound of French, Latin,
and English in which laws and statutes were written until the eighteenth
century.

two cocks in a pit, humanity cannot support it. I must
kiss all night in my own defense, and hold her down like
a boy at cuffs, nay, and give her the rising blow every
time she begins to speak.                                    95

*Enter* Rhodophil.

But here comes Rhodophil. 'Tis pretty odd that my mistress should so much resemble his: the same news-
monger, the same passionate lover of a court, the same—
But *basta,* since I must marry her, I'll say nothing, because he shall not laugh at my misfortune.                  100

RHODOPHIL.

Well, Palamede, how go the affairs of love? You've seen
your mistress?

PALAMEDE.

I have so.

RHODOPHIL.

And how, and how? Has the old Cupid your father
chosen well for you? Is he a good woodman?               105

PALAMEDE.

She's much handsomer than I could have imagined. In
short, I love her and will marry her.

RHODOPHIL.

Then you are quite off from your other mistress?

PALAMEDE.

You are mistaken; I intend to love 'em both, as a reasonable man ought to do. For, since all women have their 110
faults and imperfections, 'tis fit that one of 'em should
help out t'other.

RHODOPHIL.

This were a blessed doctrine, indeed, if our wives would

---

94. nay, and] *Q1–4, C1;* and *C2.*
108. other] *Q1–3, C1–2;* old *Q4.*
112. out t'other] *Q1–3, C2;* out the
t'other *Q4;* out 'tother *C1.*

---

92. *two cocks in a pit*] i.e., fighting in a cockpit.
94. *rising blow*] Sutherland, p. 143, suggests "upper cut," while
acknowledging the sexual joke.
99. *basta*] enough (Italian and Spanish).
105. *woodman*] hunter (*OED*).

hear it; but they're their own enemies: if they would
suffer us but now and then to make excursions, the 115
benefit of our variety would be theirs; instead of one
continued, lazy, tired love, they would in their turns have
twenty vigorous, fresh, and active loves.

PALAMEDE.

And I would ask any of 'em whether a poor narrow
brook, half dry the best part of the year and running 120
ever one way, be to be compared to a lusty stream that
has ebbs and flows?

RHODOPHIL.

Ay, or is half so profitable for navigation.

*Enter* Doralice, *walking by, and reading.*

PALAMEDE.

Ods my life, Rhodophil, will you keep my counsel?

RHODOPHIL.

Yes. Where's the secret?                          125

PALAMEDE.

There 'tis. (*Showing* Doralice.)  I may tell you as my
friend, *sub sigillo* &c., this is that very numerical lady with
whom I am in love.

RHODOPHIL *(aside).*

By all that's virtuous, my wife!

PALAMEDE.

You look strangely. How do you like her? Is she not very 130
handsome?

RHODOPHIL *(aside).*

Sure he abuses me.  (*To him.*)  Why the devil do you ask
my judgment?

PALAMEDE.

You are so dogged now, you think no man's mistress
handsome but your own. Come, you shall hear her talk 135
too; she has wit, I assure you.

---

118.  loves] *Q1–4, C1;* lovers *C2.*
121.  ever] *Q1–4, C1;* over *C2.*

---

127.  *sub sigillo*] under seal, under oath.
127.  *numerical*] identical (*OED* cites this passage).

RHODOPHIL.

This is too much, Palamede.                      *Going back.*

PALAMEDE *(pulling him forward).*

Prithee do not hang back so: of an old tried lover, thou
art the most bashful fellow!

DORALICE *(looking up).*

Were you so near and would not speak, dear husband? 140

PALAMEDE *(aside).*

Husband, quotha! I have cut out a fine piece of work for
myself.

RHODOPHIL.

Pray, spouse, how long have you been acquainted with
this gentleman?

DORALICE.

Who, I acquainted with this stranger? To my best knowl- 145
edge, I never saw him before.

*Enter* Melantha, *at the other end.*

PALAMEDE *(aside).*

Thanks, fortune, thou hast helped me.

RHODOPHIL.

Palamede, this must not pass so. I must know your mistress a little better.

PALAMEDE.

It shall be your own fault else. Come, I'll introduce you. 150

RHODOPHIL.

Introduce me! Where?

PALAMEDE.

There.

*Pointing to* Melantha, *who swiftly passes over the stage.*

To my mistress.

RHODOPHIL.

Who? Melantha! O heavens, I did not see her.

---

138. S.P. *forward*] *Q1–3, C1–2;* for-
wards *Q4.*
139. fellow!] *Q1, C1–2;* fellow,
*Q2–3;* fellow. *Q4.*
145. stranger? To] *C2;* stranger?/
To *(printed as verse) Q1–4, C1.*

151. Where?] *Q1–2, C1–2;* where!
*Q3–4.*
152.1 *after line 151 Q1–4, C1–2.*
154. Melantha! O heavens] *C2;*
Melantha!/ O heavens *(printed as*
*verse) Q1–4, C1.*

PALAMEDE.
> But I did. I am an eagle where I love; I have seen her this 155
> half hour.

DORALICE *(aside).*
> I find he has wit; he has got off so readily; but it would
> anger me if he should love Melantha.

RHODOPHIL *(aside).*
> Now I could e'en wish it were my wife he loved; I find
> he's to be married to my mistress.                    160

PALAMEDE.
> Shall I run after, and fetch her back again, to present
> you to her?

RHODOPHIL.
> No, you need not; I have the honor to have some small
> acquaintance with her.

PALAMEDE *(aside).*
> O Jupiter! what a blockhead was I not to find it out! My 165
> wife that must be is his mistress. I did a little suspect it
> before. Well, I must marry her, because she's handsome,
> and because I hate to be disinherited for a younger
> brother, which I am sure I shall be if I disobey; and yet
> must keep in with Rhodophil, because I love his 170
> wife. *(To* Rhodophil.) I must desire you to make my
> excuse to your lady if I have been so unfortunate to
> cause any mistake and, withal, to beg the honor of being
> known to her.

RHODOPHIL.
> O, that's but reason. Hark you, spouse, pray look upon 175
> this gentleman as my friend, whom, to my knowledge,
> you have never seen before this hour.

DORALICE.
> I'm so obedient a wife, sir, that my husband's commands
> shall ever be a law to me.

*Enter* Melantha *again, hastily, and runs to embrace* Doralice.

---

155. love; I] C2; love;/ I (*printed as
verse*) Q1–4, C1.

---

165. *Jupiter*] Jupiter's astrological influence includes predisposing
people to the sanguine temperament, and thus ruling the passion of love.

MELANTHA.

O, my dear, I was just going to pay my *devoirs* to you; I 180
had not time this morning, for making my court to the
king, and our new prince. Well, never nation was so
happy, and all that, in a young prince; and he's the kind-
est person in the world to me, let me die if he is not.

DORALICE.

He has been bred up far from court, and therefore— 185

MELANTHA.

That imports not: though he has not seen the *grand
monde,* and all that, let me die but he has the air of the
court, most absolutely.

PALAMEDE.

But yet, madam, he—

MELANTHA.

O, servant, you can testify that I am in his good *grâces.* 190
Well, I cannot stay long with you, because I have prom-
ised him this afternoon to—*(whispers to* Doralice*).* But
hark you, my dear, I'll tell you a secret.

RHODOPHIL *(aside).*

The devil's in me, that I must love this woman.

PALAMEDE *(aside).*

The devil's in me, that I must marry this woman.          195

MELANTHA *(raising her voice).*

So the prince and I— But you must make a secret of this,
my dear, for I would not for the world your husband
should hear it, or my tyrant, there, that must be.

PALAMEDE *(aside).*

Well, fair impertinent, your whisper is not lost, we hear
you.                                                              200

DORALICE.

I understand then, that—

MELANTHA.

I'll tell you, my dear, the prince took me by the hand and

180. *devoirs*] *this edn.;* devoirs
*Q1–4, C1–2.*
190. *grâces*] *this edn.;* graces *Q1–4,
C1–2.*

---

187. *air*] See above, II.6,7n.

pressed it *à la dérobé*, because the king was near, made
the *doux yeux* to me, and, *ensuite*, said a thousand *gallan-*
*teries*, or let me die, my dear.      205

DORALICE.

Then I am sure you—

MELANTHA.

You are mistaken, my dear.

DORALICE.

What, before I speak?

MELANTHA.

But I know your meaning; you think, my dear, that I
assumed something of *fierté* into my countenance to *re-* 210
*bute* him; but, quite contrary, I regarded him, I know not
how to express it in our dull Sicilian language, *d'un air*
*enjoué;* and said nothing but *à d'autre, à d'autre,* and that it
was all *grimace,* and would not pass upon me.

*Enter* Artemis: Melantha *sees her, and runs away from* Doralice.

*(To* Artemis.)   My dear, I must beg your pardon, I was 215
just making a loose from Doralice to pay my respects to
you. Let me die, if I ever pass time so agreeably as in
your company, and if I would leave it for any lady's in
Sicily.

ARTEMIS.

The princess Amalthea is coming this way.      220

*Enter* Amalthea; Melantha *runs to her.*

203. *à la*] *C2; al a Q1–4, C1.*
203. *dérobé*] *this edn.; derobbée Q1–3,*
*C1–2; derobbee Q4.*
204. *ensuite*] *Sutherland; in suitte*
*Q1–4, C1–2, B-B; en suitte Works.*
204–205. *gallanteries*] *Works; gal-*
lanteries *Q1–2, B-B; gallantries*
*Q3–4, C1–2, Sutherland.*
213. *à d'autre, à d'autre*] *this edn.; ad*
autre, ad autre *Q1–4, C1–2.*
215 S.D. *(To* Artemis)] *Q2–4,*
*C1–2; To Aretemis Q1.*

203. *à la dérobé*] clandestinely, by stealth, "on the sly."
203–204. *made the* doux yeux] cast amorous glances ("sweet eyes").
204. *ensuite*] then.
210. *fierté*] boldness, pride, resentment.
212–213. *d'un air enjoué*] with a spritely manner.
213. *à d'autre, à d'autre*] "Tell it to someone else, to the marines" (B-B,
p. 303).
214. *grimace*] affectation (usually, *grimaces*).
216. *making a loose*] getting away (B-B, p. 304).

MELANTHA.

O dear madam! I have been at your lodgings in my new
*calèche,* so often, to tell you of a new *amour* betwixt two
persons whom you would little suspect for it, that, let me
die if one of my coach-horses be not dead and another
quite tired and sunk under the *fatigue.*          225

AMALTHEA.

O, Melantha, I can tell you news; the prince is coming
this way.

MELANTHA.

The prince? O sweet prince! He and I are to—and I
forgot it. —Your pardon, sweet madam, for my abrupt-
ness. Adieu, my dears. —Servant, Rhodophil. —Servant, 230
servant, servant all.                    *Exit running.*

AMALTHEA (*whispers*).

Rhodophil, a word with you.

DORALICE (*to* Palamede).

Why do you not follow your mistress, sir?

PALAMEDE.

Follow her? Why, at this rate she'll be at the Indies within
this half hour.          235

DORALICE.

However, if you can't follow her all day, you'll meet her
at night, I hope?

PALAMEDE.

But can you, in charity, suffer me to be so mortified
without affording me some relief? If it be but to punish
that sign of a husband there, that lazy matrimony, that 240
dull insipid taste who leaves such delicious fare at home,
to dine abroad on worse meat, and to pay dear for't into
the bargain.

DORALICE.

All this is in vain. Assure yourself, I will never admit of
any visit from you in private.          245

228. prince?] *Sutherland;* prince,   *Q4.*
*Q1–4, C1–2.*                         237. hope?]*Q1, C1–2;* hope.*Q2–4.*
234. her?]*Q1–2, C1–2;* her!*Q3–4.*   238. be so]*Q1–3, C1–2;* be *Q4.*
236. all day] *Q1–3, C1–2;* to day

   222. *calèche*] anglicized to calash, "a kind of light carriage with low
wheels, having a removable folding hood or top" (*OED*).

PALAMEDE.

That is to tell me, in other words, my condition is desperate.

DORALICE.

I think you in so ill a condition that I am resolved to pray for you, this very evening, in the close walk behind the terrace, for that's a private place and there I am sure 250 nobody will disturb my devotions. And so, good night, sir.                                                                              *Exit.*

PALAMEDE.

This is the newest way of making an appointment I ever heard of. Let women alone to contrive the means; I find we are but dunces to 'em. Well, I will not be so profane a 255 wretch as to interrupt her devotions; but to make 'em more effectual, I'll down upon my knees and endeavor to join my own with them.                                                     *Exit.*

AMALTHEA (*to* Rhodophil).

I know already they do not love each other, and that my brother acts but a forced obedience to the king's com- 260 mands, so that if a quarrel should arise betwixt the prince and him, I were most miserable on both sides.

RHODOPHIL.

There shall be nothing wanting in me, madam, to prevent so sad a consequence.

*Enter the* King [*and*] Leonidas; *the* King *whispers* [*to*] Amalthea.

(*To himself.*) I begin to hate this Palamede, because he is 265 to marry my mistress; yet break with him I dare not, for fear of being quite excluded from her company. 'Tis a hard case when a man must go by his rival to his mistress. But 'tis at worst but using him like a pair of heavy boots in a dirty journey: after I have fouled him all day, I'll 270 throw him off at night.                                                          *Exit.*

AMALTHEA (*to the* King).

This honor is too great for me to hope.

271. S.D. *Exit.*] *Q1, C1–2; om. Q2–4.*

---

251. *good night*] Since it is the afternoon (see II. 192), Doralice's valediction holds double meaning.
259. *they*] i.e., Leonidas and Argaleon.

POLYDAMAS.

    You shall this hour have the assurance of it.
    Leonidas, come hither; you have heard,
    I doubt not, that the father of this princess        275
    Was my most faithful friend while I was yet
    A private man; and when I did assume
    This crown, he served me in that high attempt.
    You see, then, to what gratitude obliges me;
    Make your addresses to her.        280

LEONIDAS.

    Sir, I am yet too young to be a courtier;
    I should too much betray my ignorance,
    And want of breeding, to so fair a lady.

AMALTHEA.

    Your language speaks you not bred up in deserts,
    But in the softness of some Asian court        285
    Where luxury and ease invent kind words
    To cozen tender virgins of their hearts.

POLYDAMAS.

    You need not doubt
    But in what words soe'er a prince can offer
    His crown and person, they will be received.        290
    You know my pleasure, and you know your duty.

LEONIDAS.

    Yes, sir, I shall obey, in what I can.

POLYDAMAS.

    In what you can, Leonidas? Consider,
    He's both your king and father who commands you.
    Besides, what is there hard in my injunction?        295

LEONIDAS.

    'Tis hard to have my inclination forced.
    I would not marry, sir; and, when I do,
    I hope you'll give me freedom in my choice.

POLYDAMAS.

    View well this lady,
    Whose mind as much transcends her beauteous face    300
    As that excels all others.

294. you.] *Q1–3, C1–2;* you! *Q4.*

---

287. *cozen*] trick.

AMALTHEA.
    My beauty, as it ne'er could merit love,
    So neither can it beg. And, sir, you may
    Believe that what the king has offered you
    I should refuse, did I not value more          305
    Your person than your crown.

LEONIDAS.              Think it not pride
    Or my new fortunes swell me to contemn you;
    Think less that I want eyes to see your beauty;
    And least of all think duty wanting in me
    T'obey a father's will. But—

POLYDAMAS.          But what, Leonidas?    310
    For I must know your reason; and be sure
    It be convincing too.

LEONIDAS.           Sir, ask the stars,
    Which have imposed love on us like a fate,
    Why minds are bent to one, and fly another?
    Ask why all beauties cannot move all hearts?    315
    For though there may
    Be made a rule for color or for feature,
    There can be none for liking.

POLYDAMAS.
    Leonidas, you owe me more
    Than to oppose your liking to my pleasure.    320

LEONIDAS.
    I owe you all things, sir; but something too
    I owe myself.

POLYDAMAS.
    You shall dispute no more: I am a king,
    And I will be obeyed.

LEONIDAS.
    You are a king, sir, but you are no god;    325
    Or if you were, you could not force my will.

310. T'obey] *Q1–3, C1–2;* 'T obey
*Q4.*
314. to] *Q1–3, C1–2;* to the *Q4.*
315. hearts?] *Q1–4, C2;* hearts *C1.*

    326. *Or*] or else, otherwise (*OED* B4); i.e., even a god, being bound by right, could not force the natural inclination of a human will.

POLYDAMAS (*aside*).

    But you are just, you gods; O you are just
    In punishing the crimes of my rebellion
    With a rebellious son!
    Yet I can punish him, as you do me.—       330
    Leonidas, there is no jesting with
    My will. I ne'er had done so much to gain
    A crown, but to be absolute in all things.

AMALTHEA.

    O, sir, be not so much a king as to
    Forget you are a father: soft indulgence      335
    Becomes that name. Though nature gives you pow'r
    To bind his duty, 'tis with silken bonds.
    Command him, then, as you command yourself:
    He is as much a part of you as are
    Your appetite and will, and those you force not,     340
    But gently bend and make 'em pliant to your reason.

POLYDAMAS.

    It may be I have used too rough a way.
    Forgive me, my Leonidas; I know
    I lie as open to the gusts of passion
    As the bare shore to every beating surge.     345
    I will not force thee, now; but I entreat thee,
    Absolve a father's vow to this fair virgin:
    A vow which hopes of having such a son
    First caused.

LEONIDAS.

    Show not my disobedience by your pray'rs,     350
    For I must still deny you, though I now
    Appear more guilty to myself than you.
    I have some reasons which I cannot utter
    That force my disobedience; yet I mourn
    To death that the first thing you e'er enjoined me     355
    Should be that only one command in nature
    Which I could not obey.

POLYDAMAS [*aside*].

    I did descend too much below myself

---

347. *Absolve*] accomplish, perform completely (*OED* 7).

When I entreated him. —Hence, to thy desert;
Thou'rt not my son, or art not fit to be.                    360
AMALTHEA (*kneeling*).
    Great sir, I humbly beg you, make not me
    The cause of your displeasure. I absolve
    Your vow. Far, far from me be such designs,
    So wretched a desire of being great
    By making him unhappy. You may see                    365
    Something so noble in the prince's nature
    As grieves him more not to obey, than you
    That you are not obeyed.
POLYDAMAS.                    Then, for your sake
    I'll give him one day longer, to consider,
    Not to deny; for my resolves are firm                    370
    As fate, that cannot change.    *Exeunt* King *and* Amalthea.
LEONIDAS.                    And so are mine.
    This beauteous princess, charming as she is,
    Could never make me happy, I must first
    Be false to my Palmyra, and then wretched.
    But then, a father's anger!                    375
    Suppose he should recede from his own vow,
    He never would permit me to keep mine.

        *Enter* Palmyra; Argaleon *following her, a little after*.

    See, she appears!
    I'll think no more of anything but her.
    Yet I have one hour good ere I am wretched.                    380
    But, oh! Argaleon follows her! so night
    Treads on the footsteps of a winter's sun,
    And stalks all black behind him.
PALMYRA.                    O Leonidas
    (For I must call you still by that dear name),
    Free me from this bad man.                    385
LEONIDAS.
    I hope he dares not be injurious to you.

---

366. prince's] *C2*; prince his *Q1–4*,    land; consider *Q1–4, C2, Works*.
*C1*.                                                    377. would] *Q1, C1–2*; will *Q2–4*.
369. consider,] *C1, B-B, Suther-*    384. by that] *Q1–3, C1–2*; that *Q4*.

362. *absolve*] set free, pronounce free (*OED* 1).

ARGALEON.

    I rather was injurious to myself
    Than her.

LEONIDAS.

    That must be judged when I hear what you said.

ARGALEON.

    I think you need not give yourself that trouble;       390
    It concerned us alone.

LEONIDAS.

    You answer saucily and indirectly:
    What interest can you pretend in her?

ARGALEON.

    It may be, sir, I made her some expressions
    Which I would not repeat, because they were       395
    Below my rank, to one of hers.

LEONIDAS.

    What did he say, Palmyra?

PALMYRA.

    I'll tell you all. First, he began to look,
    And then he sighed, and then he looked again;
    At last, he said my eyes wounded his heart.       400
    And after that he talked of flames, and fires,
    And such strange words, that I believed he conjured.

LEONIDAS.

    O my heart! Leave me, Argaleon.

ARGALEON.

    Come, sweet Palmyra,
    I will instruct you better in my meaning.       405
    You see he would be private.

LEONIDAS.               Go yourself,
    And leave her here.

ARGALEON.          Alas, she's ignorant
    And is not fit to entertain a prince.

LEONIDAS.

    First learn what's fit for you: that's to obey.

ARGALEON.

    I know my duty is to wait on you.       410

393. interest] *Q1–3, C1–2;* intrest
*Q4.*

A great king's son, like you, ought to forget
Such mean converse.
LEONIDAS.                    What? a disputing subject?
    Hence, or my sword shall do me justice on thee.
ARGALEON (*going*).
    Yet I may find a time—
LEONIDAS (*going after him*).    What's that you mutter,
    To find a time?
ARGALEON.                —To wait on you again.—              415
    (*Softly.*)    In the meanwhile I'll watch you.
                                   *Exit, and watches during the scene.*

LEONIDAS.
    How precious are the hours of love in courts!
    In cottages, where love has all the day,
    Full, and at ease, he throws it half away.
    Time gives himself, and is not valued, there,          420
    But sells at mighty rates each minute here.
    There, he is lazy, unemployed, and slow;
    Here, he's more swift, and yet has more to do.
    So many of his hours in public move,
    That few are left for privacy and love.                425

PALMYRA.
    The sun, methinks, shines faint and dimly, here;
    Light is not half so long, nor half so clear.
    But oh! when every day was yours and mine,
    How early up! what haste he made to shine!

LEONIDAS.                                                    430
    Such golden days no prince must hope to see,
    Whose ev'ry subject is more blessed than he.

PALMYRA.
    Do you remember, when their tasks were done,
    How all the youth did to our cottage run?
    While winter winds were whistling loud without,
    Our cheerful hearth was circled round about:            435
    With strokes in ashes maids their lovers drew,
    And still you fell to me, and I to you.

---

436. *With strokes . . . drew*] "The maidens gathered about the hearth,
and in the ashes which had fallen from the fire made marks or strokes,
which, with a little imagination, could be easily interpreted as the initials
of their lovers" (Sutherland, p. 143).

LEONIDAS.

> When love did of my heart possession take,
> I was so young, my soul was scarce awake.
> I cannot tell when first I thought you fair,                    440
> But sucked in love insensibly as air.

PALMYRA.

> I know too well when first my love began,
> When, at our wake, you for the chaplet ran.
> Then I was made the lady of the May
> And with the garland at the goal did stay.                      445
> Still, as you ran, I kept you full in view;
> I hoped, and wished, and ran, methought, for you.
> As you came near, I hastily did rise,
> And stretched my arm outright that held the prize.
> The custom was to kiss whom I should crown:                     450
> You kneeled and, in my lap, your head laid down.
> I blushed, and blushed, and did the kiss delay:
> At last my subjects forced me to obey;
> But, when I gave the crown, and then the kiss,
> I scarce had breath to say, take that—and this.                 455

LEONIDAS.

> I felt the while a pleasing kind of smart;
> The kiss went, tingling, to my very heart.
> When it was gone, the sense of it did stay; ⎤
> The sweetness clinged upon my lips all day ⎬
> Like drops of honey, loath to fall away. ⎦                      460

PALMYRA.

> Life, like a prodigal, gave all his store
> To my first youth, and now can give no more.
> You are a prince, and in that high degree,
> No longer must converse with humble me.

LEONIDAS.

> 'Twas to my loss the gods that title gave;                      465

457. my very] *Q1–3, C1–2; my Q4.*

---

443. *wake*] local annual festival.
443. *chaplet*] garland, crown of flowers.
445. *stay*] wait.
446. *Still*] always.
449. *outright*] straight ahead.

A tyrant's son is doubly born a slave:
He gives a crown, but, to prevent my life
From being happy, loads it with a wife.

PALMYRA.

Speak quickly: what have you resolved to do?

LEONIDAS.

To keep my faith inviolate to you.                          470
He threatens me with exile, and with shame,
To lose my birthright, and a prince's name;
But there's a blessing which he did not mean,
To send me back to love and you again.

PALMYRA.

Why was not I a princess for your sake?                     475
But heav'n no more such miracles can make.
And, since that cannot, this must never be;
You shall not lose a crown for love of me.
Live happy, and a nobler choice pursue;
I shall complain of fate, but not of you.                   480

LEONIDAS.

Can you so easily without me live?
Or could you take the counsel which you give?
Were you a princess would you not be true?

PALMYRA.

I would, but cannot merit it from you.

LEONIDAS.

Did you not merit, as you do, my heart?                     485
Love gives esteem, and then it gives desert.
But if I basely could forget my vow,
Poor helpless innocence, what would you do?

PALMYRA.

In woods and plains where first my love began,
There would I live, retired from faithless man.             490
I'd sit all day within some lonely shade,
Or that close arbor which your hands have made.
I'd search the groves, and ev'ry tree, to find

472.  prince's] C2; prince his Q1–4,     Q1; heav n C2.
C1.                                      485.  heart?] this edn.; heart; Q1–4,
476.  heav'n] Q2–4, C1; heav'en          C1–2.

486. *desert*] deserving, excellence, worth.

Where you had carved our names upon the rind.
Your hook, your scrip, all that was yours, I'd keep,          495
And lay 'em by me when I went to sleep.
Thus would I live: and maidens, when I die,
Upon my hearse white true-love knots should tie.
And thus my tomb should be inscribed above,
"Here the forsaken virgin rests from love."                  500

LEONIDAS.

Think not that time or fate shall e'er divide
Those hearts, which love and mutual vows have tied.
But we must part: farewell, my love.

PALMYRA.                                   Till when?

LEONIDAS.

Till the next age of hours we meet again.
Meantime—we may,                                            505
When near each other we in public stand,
Contrive to catch a look, or steal a hand:
Fancy will ev'ry touch and glance improve,
And draw the most spirituous parts of love.
  Our souls sit close and silently within,                  510
  And their own web from their own entrails spin.
  And when eyes meet far off, our sense is such
  That, spider-like, we feel the tender'st touch.   *Exeunt.*

508. ev'ry] *this edn.;* every *Q1–4,*
*C1–2.*

---

495. *hook . . . scrip*] shepherd's crook and wallet.
  502. *love and mutual vows have tied*] Even private mutual vows "had the
validity of a public marriage ceremony" (*Works,* 11:498).

# ACT III

[III.i] *Enter* Rhodophil, *meeting* Doralice *and* Artemis.
Rhodophil *and* Doralice *embrace*.

RHODOPHIL.
    My own dear heart!
DORALICE.
    My own true love! (*She starts back*.)  I had forgot myself
    to be so kind; indeed I am very angry with you, dear; you
    are come home an hour after you appointed. If you had
    stayed a minute longer, I was just considering whether I    5
    should stab, hang, or drown myself.

                                          *Embracing him*.

RHODOPHIL.
    Nothing but the king's business could have hindered me;
    and I was so vexed that I was just laying down my
    commission rather than have failed my dear.

                                          *Kissing her hand*.

ARTEMIS.
    Why, this is love as it should be betwixt man and wife:    10
    such another couple would bring marriage into fashion
    again. But is it always thus betwixt you?
RHODOPHIL.
    Always thus! this is nothing. I tell you there is not such a
    pair of turtles in all Sicily; there is such an eternal cooing
    and kissing betwixt us, that indeed it is scandalous before    15
    civil company.
DORALICE.
    Well, if I had imagined I should have been this fond
    fool, I would never have married the man I loved. I
    married to be happy, and have made myself miserable by
    over-loving. Nay, and now, my case is desperate; for I    20
    have been married above these two years and find myself
    every day worse and worse in love: nothing but madness
    can be the end on't.

---

9. have failed] *Q1–4, C2;* fail *C1*.          12. you?] *Q1–3, C1–2;* you! *Q4*.
9.1. *Kissing*] *Q1–4, C1; Kisses C2*.

---

14. *turtles*] turtledoves, lovers.

ARTEMIS.

Dote on, to the extremity, and you are happy.

DORALICE.

He deserves so infinitely much that, the truth is, there      25
can be no doting in the matter; but to love well, I confess, is a work that pays itself: 'tis telling gold, and after,
taking it for one's pains.

RHODOPHIL.

By that I should be a very covetous person, for I am ever
pulling out my money and putting it into my pocket      30
again.

DORALICE.

O dear Rhodophil!

RHODOPHIL.

O sweet Doralice!                    *Embracing each other.*

ARTEMIS (*aside*).

Nay, I am resolved, I'll never interrupt lovers: I leave
'em as happy as I found 'em.            *Steals away.*   35

RHODOPHIL (*looking up*).

What, is she gone?

DORALICE.

Yes; and without taking leave.

RHODOPHIL (*parting from her*).

Then there's enough for this time.

DORALICE.

Yes sure, the scene's done, I take it.

*They walk contrary ways on the stage; he, with his hands in his pocket,*
*whistling; she, singing a dull melancholy tune.*

RHODOPHIL.

Pox o' your dull tune; a man can't think for you.            40

DORALICE.

Pox o' your damned whistling; you can neither be company to me yourself, nor leave me to the freedom of my
own fancy.

34. I am] *Q1–2, C1–2;* I'm *Q3–4.*
38. time.] *Q2–4, C1–2;* time *Q1.*
43. own] *Q1–3, C1–2;* one *Q4.*

27. *telling*] counting.

RHODOPHIL.

Well, thou art the most provoking wife!

DORALICE.

Well, thou art the dullest husband; thou art never to be    45
provoked.

RHODOPHIL.

I was never thought dull till I married thee; and now
thou hast made an old knife of me; thou hast whetted me
so long, till I have no edge left.

DORALICE.

I see you are in the husband's fashion; you reserve all    50
your good humors for your mistresses, and keep your ill
for your wives.

RHODOPHIL.

Prithee leave me to my own cogitations; I am thinking
over all my sins, to find for which of them it was I married thee.                                                 55

DORALICE.

Whatever your sin was, mine's the punishment.

RHODOPHIL.

My comfort is thou art not immortal; and when that
blessed, that divine day comes of thy departure, I'm resolved I'll make one holy-day more in the almanac for
thy sake.                                                   60

DORALICE.

Ay, you had need make a holy-day for me, for I am sure
you have made me a martyr.

RHODOPHIL.

Then, setting my victorious foot upon thy head, in the
first hour of thy silence (that is, the first hour thou art
dead, for I despair of it before), I will swear by thy ghost,    65
an oath as terrible to me as Styx is to the gods, never
more to be in danger of the banes of matrimony.

46. provoked.] *Q2–4, C1–2;* provoked, *Q1.*
50. husband's] *Sutherland;* husbands *Q1–4, C1–2.*
54. it was I] *Q1–3, C1–2;* I *Q4.*

59, 61. holy-day] *Q1–4, C1–2;*
hol-iday *Sutherland.*
65. thy] *Q1–2, C1–2;* the *Q3–4.*
67. in] *Q1–3, C1–2;* in the *Q4.*

67. *banes*] "Banes" is an obsolete spelling for "banns," published
announcement of a proposed wedding; but the pun is intended.

DORALICE.

> And I am resolved to marry the very same day thou
> die'st, if it be but to show how little I'm concerned for
> thee. 70

RHODOPHIL.

> Prithee, Doralice, why do we quarrel thus a-days? ha?
> This is but a kind of heathenish life and does not answer
> the ends of marriage. If I have erred, propound what
> reasonable atonement may be made, before we sleep,
> and I shall not be refractory: but withal consider, I have 75
> been married these three years, and be not too tyran-
> nical.

DORALICE.

> What should you talk of peace abed, when you can give
> no security for performance of articles?

RHODOPHIL.

> Then, since we must live together, and both of us stand 80
> upon our terms, as to the matter of dying first, let us
> make ourselves as merry as we can with our misfortunes.
>
> Why there's the devil on't! If thou couldst make my
> enjoying thee but a little less easy, or a little more unlawful,
> thou shouldst see what a termagant lover I would prove. 85
> I have taken such pains to enjoy thee, Doralice, that I have
> fancied thee all the fine women in the town to help me out.
> But now there's none left for me to think on, my imagina-
> tion is quite jaded. Thou art a wife, and thou wilt be a wife,
> and I can make thee another no longer. 90

> *Exit* Rhodophil.

DORALICE.

> Well, since thou art a husband, and wilt be a husband, I'll
> try if I can find out another! 'Tis a pretty time we women
> have on't, to be made widows while we are married. Our
> husbands think it reasonable to complain that we are the
> same, and the same to them, when we have more reason 95
> to complain that they are not the same to us. Because

69. be but] *Q1, C1–2,* be *Q2–4.*      86. taken] *Q1–4, C2;* take *C1.*
71. ha?] *Q1–2, C1–2;* ha! *Q3–4.*      90. thee] *Q1–2, C1–2;* the *Q3–4.*
78. What] *Q1–2, C1–2;* Why *Q3–4.*
84. or a] *Q1–3, C1–2;* or but a *Q4.*

they cannot feed on one dish, therefore we must be
starved. 'Tis enough that they have a sufficient ordinary
provided and a table ready spread for 'em: if they cannot
fall to and eat heartily, the fault is theirs; and 'tis pity, 100
methinks, that the good creature should be lost when
many a poor sinner would be glad on't.

*Enter* Melantha *and* Artemis *to her.*

MELANTHA.

Dear, my dear, pity me; I am so *chagrin* today, and have
had the most signal affront at court! I went this afternoon to do my *devoir* to princess Amalthea, found her, 105
conversed with her, and helped to make her court some
half an hour, after which she went to take the air, chose
out two ladies to go with her that came in after me, and
left me most barbarously behind her.

ARTEMIS.

You are the less to be pitied, Melantha, because you 110
subject yourself to these affronts by coming perpetually
to court, where you have no business nor employment.

MELANTHA.

I declare, I had rather of the two be *rallied,* nay *mal
traittée* at court, than be deified in the town; for assuredly
nothing can be so *ridicule* as a mere town lady.          115

DORALICE.

Especially at court. How I have seen 'em crowd and
sweat in the drawing room on a holiday night! For that's
their time to swarm and invade the presence. O, how
they catch at a bow or any little salute from a courtier to
make show of their acquaintance! and rather than be 120
thought to be quite unknown, they curtsy to one
another. But they take true pains to come near the circle,
and press and peep upon the princess, to write letters
into the country how she was dressed, while the ladies
that stand about make their court to her with abusing 125
them.

97. we] *Q1–3, C1–2;* wee *Q4.*          105. *devoir*] *this edn.;* devoir *Q1–4,*
100. to] *Q4;* too *Q1–3, C1–2.*          *C1–2.*

98. *ordinary*] tavern or eating house providing meals to all comers.

– 56 –

ARTEMIS.

These are sad truths, Melantha; and therefore I would
e'en advise you to quit the court and live either wholly in
the town or, if you like not that, in the country.

DORALICE.

In the country! nay, that's to fall beneath the town, for 130
they live there upon our offals here: their entertainment
of wit is only the remembrance of what they had when
they were last in town; they live this year upon the last
year's knowledge, as their cattle do all night by chewing
the cud of what they ate in the afternoon.                    135

MELANTHA.

And they tell for news such unlikely stories; a letter from
one of us is such a present to 'em that the poor souls wait
for the carrier's day with such devotion that they cannot
sleep the night before.

ARTEMIS.

No more than I can the night before I am to go a jour- 140
ney.

DORALICE.

Or I, before I am to try on a new gown.

MELANTHA.

A song that's stale here will be new there a twelve-month
hence; and if a man of the town by chance come amongst
'em, he's reverenced for teaching 'em the tune.              145

DORALICE.

A friend of mine, who makes songs sometimes, came
lately out of the west and vowed he was so put out of
countenance with a song of his; for at the first country
gentleman's he visited, he saw three tailors cross-legged
upon the table in the hall, who were tearing out as loud 150
as ever they could sing,
        —"After the pangs of a desperate lover, etc."

133. upon the] *Q1–3, C1–2;* upon
*Q4.*
135. ate] *this edn.;* eat *(i.e., past
tense) Q1–4, C1–2.*

138. *carrier's*] mail carrier's.
152. *"After . . . etc."*] a song by Dryden in *An Evening's Love* (1668).

and all that day he heard nothing else but the daughters
of the house and the maids humming it over in every
corner and the father whistling it.                                    155

ARTEMIS.

Indeed I have observed of myself that when I am out of
town but a fortnight, I am so humble that I would receive a letter from my tailor or mercer for a favor.

MELANTHA.

When I have been at grass in the summer and am new
come up again, methinks I'm to be turned into *ridicule* by 160
all that see me; but when I have been once or twice at
court, I begin to value myself again and to despise my
country acquaintance.

ARTEMIS.

There are places where all people may be adored, and
we ought to know ourselves so well as to choose 'em.      165

DORALICE.

That's very true. Your little courtier's wife, who speaks to
the king but once a month, need but go to a town lady,
and there she may vapor and cry "the king and I" at
every word. Your town lady, who is laughed at in the
circle, takes her coach into the city, and there she's called 170
"your honor" and has a banquet from the merchant's
wife, whom she laughs at for her kindness. And, as for
my finical cit, she removes but to her country house and
there insults over the country gentlewoman that never
comes up, who treats her with frumity and custard, and 175

---

160. I'm] *Q1–3, C1–2;* I am *Q4.*          *Q2;* town lady; *Q1, C1–2.*
165. 'em] *Q1–4, C1;* them *C2.*            174. there] *Q1, Q4, C1–2;* their
167. town lady,] *Q3–4;* town lady       *Q2–3.*

---

159. *at grass*] in the country.

160. *come up*] i.e., to town.

168. *vapor*] bluster, brag, boast (*OED*).

170. *city*] the older, predominantly mercantile center of London;
much fun was made of the area and its inhabitants, who were opprobri-
ously known as "cits."

173. *finical*] over-nice or particular, affectedly fastidious (*OED*).

173. *cit*] See III.i.170 n.

175. *frumity*] sweetened creamed wheat.

opens her dear bottle of *mirabilis* beside, for a gill-glass of
it at parting.

ARTEMIS.

At last, I see, we shall leave Melantha where we found
her; for, by your description of the town and country,
they are become more dreadful to her than the court  180
where she was affronted. But you forget we are to wait
on the princess Amalthea. Come, Doralice.

DORALICE.

Farewell, Melantha.

MELANTHA.

Adieu, my dear.

ARTEMIS.

You are out of charity with her, and therefore I shall not  185
give your service.

MELANTHA.

Do not omit it, I beseech you; for I have such a *tendre* for
the court that I love it ev'n from the drawing room to the
lobby and can never be *rebutée* by any usage. But, hark
you, my dears, one thing I had forgot of great con-  190
cernment.

DORALICE.

Quickly then, we are in haste.

MELANTHA.

Do not call it my "service," that's too vulgar; but do my
*baise-mains* to the princess Amalthea: that is *spirituelle*!

DORALICE.

To do you service then, we will *pendre* the *carrosse* to  195
court, and do your *baise-mains* to the princess Amalthea,
in your phrase, *spirituelle*.          *Exeunt* Artemis *and* Doralice.

*Enter* Philotis, *with a paper in her hand.*

MELANTHA.

O, are you there, minion? And, well, are not you a most

196. do] *Q1–3, C1–2;* to do *Q4.*

___

176. *mirabilis*] *aqua mirabilis* ("wonderful water"), a mixture of wine
and spices.
176. *gill-glass*] glass holding four ounces.
195. *carrosse*] coach.

precious damsel, to retard all my visits for want of language, when you know you are paid so well for fur- 200
nishing me with new words for my daily conversation?
Let me die, if I have not run the *risque* already to speak
like one of the vulgar, and if I have one phrase left in all
my store that is not threadbare and *usé* and fit for nothing but to be thrown to peasants.                         205

PHILOTIS.

Indeed, madam, I have been very diligent in my voca-
tion, but you have so drained all the French plays and
romances that they are not able to supply you with words
for your daily expenses.

MELANTHA.

Drained? what a word's there! *Épuisée,* you sot you. 210
Come, produce your morning's work.

PHILOTIS.

'Tis here, madam.                              *Shows the paper.*

MELANTHA.

O, my Venus! fourteen or fifteen words to serve me a
whole day! Let me die, at this rate I cannot last till night.
Come, read your works: twenty to one half of 'em will 215
not pass muster neither.

PHILOTIS (*reads*).

*Sottises.*

MELANTHA.

*Sottises: bon.* That's an excellent word to begin withal: as,
for example, he or she said a thousand *sottises* to me.
Proceed.                                                 220

PHILOTIS.

*Figure,* as what a *figure* of a man is there! *Naive,* and
*naiveté*.

MELANTHA.

*Naive!* as how?

209. expenses] *Q1–4, C1;* expense
*C2.*
210. *Épuisée] C1–2; begins new par-*
*agraph Q1–4.*
215. works] *Q1–4, C1–2,* Sutherland, B-B; words *Works.*
215. 'em] *Q1–3, C1–2;* them *Q4.*
219. to me] *Q1–4, C2;* me *C1.*
221. *Naive] C1; begins new para-*
*graph Q1–4, C2.*

215. *works*] labors (B-B, p. 316).
217. *Sottises*] foolishness, nonsense.

PHILOTIS.

Speaking of a thing that was naturally said: It was so *naive*, or such an innocent piece of simplicity; 'twas such 225 a *naiveté*.

MELANTHA.

Truce with your interpretations: make haste.

PHILOTIS.

*Foible, chagrin, grimace, embarrassé, double entendre, équivoque, éclaircissement, suite, bévue, façon, penchant, coup d'étourdi,* and *ridicule*. 230

MELANTHA.

Hold, hold: how did they begin?

PHILOTIS.

They began at *sottises* and ended *en ridicule*.

MELANTHA.

Now give me your paper in my hand and hold you my glass while I practice my postures for the day.

        Melantha *laughs in the glass.*

How does that laugh become my face? 235

PHILOTIS.

Sovereignly well, madam.

MELANTHA.

Sovereignly! Let me die, that's not amiss. That word shall not be yours; I'll invent it and bring it up myself: my new point gorget shall be yours upon't. Not a word of the word, I charge you. 240

PHILOTIS.

I am dumb, madam.

MELANTHA (*looking in the glass again*).

That glance, how suits it with my face?

PHILOTIS.

'Tis so *languissant*.

MELANTHA.

*Languissant!* that word shall be mine too, and my last

---

229. *éclaircissement, suite, bévue*] explanation, elucidation; retinue, attendants; blunder, oversight.

229–230. *coup d'étourdi*] heedlessness, thoughtlessness, giddy act.

239. *point gorget*] lace wimple, a covering for the neck and breast (*OED*).

Indian gown thine for't.  (*Looks again.*)   That sigh?      245
PHILOTIS.

'Twill make many a man sigh, madam. 'Tis a mere in-
cendiary.

MELANTHA.

Take my gimp petticoat for that truth. If thou hast more
of these phrases, let me die but I could give away all my
wardrobe and go naked for 'em.                                  250

PHILOTIS.

Go naked? then you would be a Venus, madam. O Jupiter! what had I forgot? This paper was given me by
Rhodophil's page.

MELANTHA (*reading the letter*).

"Beg the favor from you—gratify my passion—so far—
assignation—in the grotto—behind the terrace—clock 255
this evening—" Well, for the *billets-doux* there's no man in
Sicily must dispute with Rhodophil; they are so French,
so *gallant*, and so *tendre*, that I cannot resist the temptation of the assignation. Now go you away, Philotis; it
imports me to practice what I shall say to my servant 260
when I meet him.                                    *Exit* Philotis.
"Rhodophil, you'll wonder at my assurance to meet you
here; let me die, I am so out of breath with coming that I
can render you no reason of it." Then he will make this
*repartie*: "Madam, I have no reason to accuse you for that 265
which is so great a favor to me." Then I reply, "But why
have you drawn me to this solitary place? let me die but I
am apprehensive of some violence from you." Then, says
he, "Solitude, madam, is most fit for lovers; but by this
fair hand—" "—Nay, now I vow you're rude, sir. O fie, 270
fie, fie; I hope you'll be honorable?—" "—You'd laugh at

254. you—] *Q2–4, C1;* you.—*Q1,*
*C2.*
256. there's] *Q1–4, C1;* there is *C2.*
270. rude,] *Q3–4, C1–2;* rude.
*Q1–2.*

245. *Indian gown*] a gaudy dressing gown of Indian cloth.
246. *mere*] absolute, sheer, perfect (*OED*).
248. *gimp petticoat*] patterned lace outer skirt.
264. *render*] Perhaps Melantha says "*rendre*," to render, emit.

me if I should, madam—" "—What do you mean to
throw me down thus? Ah me! ah, ah, ah."

*Enter* Polydamas, Leonidas, *and Guards.*

O Venus! the king and court. Let me die but I fear they
have found my *foible* and will turn me into *ridicule.*          275

*Exit running.*

LEONIDAS.
    Sir, I beseech you.
POLYDAMAS.                    Do not urge my patience.
LEONIDAS.
    I'll not deny
    But what your spies informed you of is true:
    I love the fair Palmyra, but I loved her
    Before I knew your title to my blood.          280

*Enter* Palmyra, *guarded.*

    See, here she comes, and looks, amidst her guards,
    Like a weak dove under the falcon's gripe.
    O heav'n, I cannot bear it.
POLYDAMAS.                    Maid, come hither.
    Have you presumed so far as to receive
    My son's affection?          285
PALMYRA.
    Alas, what shall I answer? To confess it
    Will raise a blush upon a virgin's face;
    Yet I was ever taught 'twas base to lie.
POLYDAMAS.
    You've been too bold, and you must love no more.
PALMYRA.
    Indeed I must; I cannot help my love;          290
    I was so tender when I took the bent
    That now I grow that way.
POLYDAMAS.
    He is a prince, and you are meanly born.

273. ah, ah, ah] *Q1, C1–2;* ha, ha,
ha *Q2–4.*
279. the] *Q1–3, C1–2;* this *Q4.*

_____

272. *What*] Why *(OED).* The action is completed in Melantha's imagination (Sutherland, p. 145).

LEONIDAS.

> Love either finds equality, or makes it:
> Like death, he knows no difference in degrees,     295
> But planes and levels all.

PALMYRA.

> Alas, I had not rendered up my heart
> Had he not loved me first; but he preferred me
> Above the maidens of my age and rank,
> Still shunned their company, and still sought mine.     300
> I was not won by gifts, yet still he gave;
> And all his gifts, though small, yet spoke his love.
> He picked the earliest strawberries in woods,
> The clustered filberts, and the purple grapes.
> He taught a prating stare to speak my name;     305
> And when he found a nest of nightingales
> Or callow linnets, he would show 'em me,
> And let me take 'em out.

POLYDAMAS.

> This is a little mistress, meanly born,
> Fit only for a prince's vacant hours,     310
> And then, to laugh at her simplicity,
> Not fix a passion there. Now hear my sentence.

LEONIDAS.

> Remember, ere you give it, 'tis pronounced
> Against us both.

POLYDAMAS.

> First, in her hand     315
> There shall be placed a player's painted scepter,
> And on her head a gilded pageant crown;
> Thus shall she go,
> With all the boys attending on her triumph:
> That done, be put alone into a boat,     320
> With bread and water only for three days,

---

304. and the] *Q1, C1–2;* and *Q2–4.*
310. prince's] *C2;* prince his *Q1–4,*
*C1.*

---

300. *Still*] always.
305. *stare*] starling.
307. *linnets*] Old World species of finch.

So on the sea she shall be set adrift,
And who relieves her, dies.

PALMYRA.

I only beg that you would execute
The last part first: let me be put to sea;                    325
The bread and water for my three days' life
I give you back; I would not live so long;
But let me 'scape the shame.

LEONIDAS.

Look to me, piety;
And you, O gods, look to my piety:                    330
Keep me from saying that which misbecomes a son;
But let me die before I see this done.

POLYDAMAS.

If you forever will abjure her sight,
I can be yet a father; she shall live.

LEONIDAS.

Hear, O you pow'rs, is this to be a father?                    335
I see 'tis all my happiness and quiet
You aim at, sir; and take 'em:
I will not save ev'n my Palmyra's life
At that ignoble price; but I'll die with her.

PALMYRA.

So had I done by you                    340
Had fate made me a princess. Death, methinks,
Is not a terror now;
He is not fierce or grim, but fawns and soothes me,
And slides along, like Cleopatra's aspic,
Off'ring his service to my troubled breast.                    345

LEONIDAS.

Begin what you have purposed when you please;
Lead her to scorn, your triumph shall be doubled.

---

329–330. Look . . . piety;/And          345. troubled] *Q1, Q3–4, C1–2;*
. . . piety] *Sutherland, B-B, Works;*          trouled *Q2.*
*one line Q1–4, C1–2.*

---

329–330. *piety . . . piety*] "Leonidas seems to use the word first in the
sense of 'Virtue' to refer to Palmyra, and then in reference to his filial duty
to Polydamas" (*Works,* 11:499).

344. *Cleopatra's aspic*] the asp by whose means Cleopatra committed
suicide.

As holy priests
In pity go with dying malefactors,
So will I share her shame.                                            350

POLYDAMAS.

You shall not have your will so much; first part 'em,
Then execute your office.

LEONIDAS.                            No, I'll die
In her defense.                              *Draws his sword.*

PALMYRA.          Ah, hold, and pull not on
A curse, to make me worthy of my death;
Do not by lawless force oppose your father,            355
Whom you have too much disobeyed for me.

LEONIDAS.

Here, take it, sir, and with it pierce my heart.

*Presenting his sword to his father upon his knees.*

You have done more in taking my Palmyra.
You are my father, therefore I submit.

POLYDAMAS.

Keep him from anything he may design                 360
Against his life whilst the first fury lasts;
And now perform what I commanded you.

LEONIDAS.

In vain; if sword and poison be denied me,
I'll hold my breath and die.

PALMYRA.

Farewell, my last Leonidas; yet live,                      365
I charge you live, till you believe me dead.
I cannot die in peace if you die first.
If life's a blessing, you shall have it last.

POLYDAMAS.

Go on with her, and lead him after me.

*Enter* Argaleon *hastily, with* Hermogenes.

353. S.D. *sword*] *Q1, Q3–4, C1–2;*
*sowrd Q2.*

363–364. *if . . . die*] "For similar threats of heroic self control see
Indamora in *Aureng-Zebe* V.i, Don Sebastian in *Don Sebastian* V.i, and
Cleonidas in *Cleomenes* IV.i" (*Works,* 11:499).

ARGALEON.

I bring you, sir, such news as must amaze you,          370
And such as will prevent you from an action
Which would have rendered all your life unhappy.

*Hermogenes kneels.*

POLYDAMAS.

Hermogenes, you bend your knees in vain,
My doom's already past.

HERMOGENES.

I kneel not for Palmyra, for I know          375
She will not need my prayers, but for myself:
With a feigned tale I have abused your ears
And therefore merit death; but since, unforced,
I first accuse myself, I hope your mercy.

POLYDAMAS.

Haste to explain your meaning.          380

HERMOGENES.

Then, in few words, Palmyra is your daughter.

POLYDAMAS.

How can I give belief to this imposter?
He who has once abused me, often may.
I'll hear no more.

ARGALEON.          For your own sake, you must.

HERMOGENES.

A parent's love (for I confess my crime)          385
Moved me to say Leonidas was yours;
But when I heard Palmyra was to die,
The fear of guiltless blood so stung my conscience
That I resolved, even with my shame, to save
Your daughter's life.          390

POLYDAMAS.

But how can I be certain but that interest,
Which moved you first to say your son was mine,
Does not now move you too to save your daughter?

HERMOGENES.

You had but then my word; I bring you now
Authentic testimonies. Sir, in short,          395

383. has once] *Q1–3, C1–2;* once    391. but that] *Q1–4, C2;* that that
has *Q4.*                                      *C1.*

– 67 –

*Delivers on his knees a jewel, and a letter.*

If this will not convince you, let me suffer.

POLYDAMAS.

I know this jewel well; 'twas once my mother's,

*Looking first on the jewel.*

Which, marrying, I presented to my wife.
And this, O this, is my Eudocia's hand.
(*Reads.*)   "This was the pledge of love given to Eudocia, 400
Who, dying, to her young Palmyra leaves it.
And this when you, my dearest lord, receive,
Own her, and think on me, dying Eudocia."
(*To* Argaleon.)  Take it; 'tis well there is no more to read,
My eyes grow full and swim in their own light.          405

*He embraces* Palmyra.

PALMYRA.

I fear, sir, this is your intended pageant.
You sport yourself at poor Palmyra's cost.
But if you think to make me proud,
Indeed I cannot be so: I was born
With humble thoughts, and lowly, like my birth.          410
A real fortune could not make me haughty,
Much less a feigned.

POLYDAMAS.                    This was her mother's temper.
I have too much deserved thou shouldst suspect
That I am not thy father; but my love
Shall henceforth show I am. Behold my eyes,              415
And see a father there begin to flow:
This is not feigned, Palmyra.

PALMYRA.

I doubt no longer, sir; you are a king
And cannot lie: falsehood's a vice too base
To find a room in any royal breast.                      420

---

397. this] *Q1, C1–2;* the *Q2–4.*     *C1–2, Works;* Eudoxia *Sutherland,*
397.1. *Looking*] *Q1, Q3–4, C1–2;*     *B-B.*
*Lookin Q2.*                            405. their] *Q1–3;* there *Q4, C1–2.*
399,  400,  403. Eudocia] *Q1–4,*

---

399, 400, 403. *Eudocia*] See Introduction, p. xiv.

I know, in spite of my unworthiness,
I am your child; for when you would have killed me,
Methought I loved you then.

ARGALEON.

Sir, we forget the prince Leonidas,
His greatness should not stand neglected thus.                425

POLYDAMAS.

Guards, you may now retire. Give him his sword,
And leave him free.

LEONIDAS.

Then the first use I make of liberty
Shall be, with your permission, mighty sir,
To pay that reverence to which nature binds me.             430

                                    *Kneels to* Hermogenes.

ARGALEON.

Sure you forget your birth, thus to misplace
This act of your obedience; you should kneel
To nothing but to heav'n, and to a king.

LEONIDAS.

I never shall forget what nature owes,
Nor be ashamed to pay it; though my father                  435
Be not a king, I know him brave and honest,
And well deserving of a worthier son.

POLYDAMAS.

He bears it gallantly.

LEONIDAS (*to* Hermogenes).

Why would you not instruct me, sir, before,
Where I should place my duty?                                440
From which, if ignorance have made me swerve,
I beg your pardon for an erring son.

PALMYRA.

I almost grieve I am a princess, since
It makes him lose a crown.

LEONIDAS.

And next, to you, my king, thus low I kneel,               445
T'implore your mercy; if in that small time
I had the honor to be thought your son

424. forget] *Q1,  C1–2;*  forgot
*Q2–4.*

I paid not strict obedience to your will,
I thought, indeed, I should not be compelled,
But thought it as your son; so what I took          450
In duty from you, I restored in courage,
Because your son should not be forced.

POLYDAMAS.

You have my pardon for it.

LEONIDAS.

To you, fair princess, I congratulate
Your birth, of which I ever thought you worthy.          455
And give me leave to add, that I am proud
The gods have picked me out to be the man
By whose dejected fate yours is to rise,
Because no man could more desire your fortune,
Or franklier part with his to make you great.          460

PALMYRA.

I know the king, though you are not his son,
Will still regard you as my foster-brother,
And so conduct you downward from a throne
By slow degrees, so unperceived and soft
That it may seem no fall, or, if it be,          465
May fortune lay a bed of down beneath you.

POLYDAMAS.

He shall be ranked with my nobility,
And kept from scorn by a large pension given him.

LEONIDAS (*bowing*).

You are all great and royal in your gifts;
But at the donor's feet I lay 'em down:          470
Should I take riches from you, it would seem
As I did want a soul to bear that poverty
To which the gods designed my humble birth.
And should I take your honors without merit,
It would appear I wanted manly courage          475
To hope 'em, in your service, from my sword.

POLYDAMAS.

Still brave and like yourself.

459. your] *Q1–2, C1–2;* you *Q3–4.*     462. regard] *Q1, Q3–4, C1–2;* re-
461. you] *Q1–2, Q4, C1–2;* your     guard *Q2.*
*Q3.*

The court shall shine this night in its full splendor,
And celebrate this new discovery.
Argaleon, lead my daughter: as we go                    480
I shall have time to give her my commands,
In which you are concerned.

*Exeunt all but* Leonidas.

LEONIDAS.

Methinks I do not want
That huge long train of fawning followers
That swept a furlong after me.                    485
'Tis true, I am alone;
So was the godhead ere he made the world,
And better served himself than served by nature.
And yet I have a soul
Above this humble fate. I could command,                    490
Love to do good, give largely to true merit—
All that a king should do. But though these are not
My province, I have scene enough within
To exercise my virtue.

All that a heart, so fixed as mine, can move,                    495
Is, that my niggard fortune starves my love.                    *Exit.*

[III.ii]

Palamede *and* Doralice *meet: she, with a book in her hand, seems to start at sight of him.*

DORALICE.

'Tis a strange thing that no warning will serve your turn,
and that no retirement will secure me from your impertinent addresses! Did I not tell you that I was to be private here at my devotions?

PALAMEDE.

Yes, and you see I have observed my cue exactly. I am                    5
come to relieve you from them. Come, shut up, shut up
your book; the man's come who is to supply all your
necessities.

---

486. alone] *Q1, Q4, C1–2;* lone *Q2–3.*
493. scene] *Q1, C1–2;* seen *Q2–4.*

0.2. S.D. *at] Q1–4, C1; at the C2.*
5. exactly] *Q1, Q3–4, C1–2;* axactly *Q2.*

---

483. *want*] lack, miss having.

DORALICE.

Then, it seems, you are so impudent to think it was an assignation? This, I warrant, was your lewd interpreta-  10
tion of my innocent meaning.

PALAMEDE.

Venus forbid that I should harbor so unreasonable a thought of a fair young lady, that you should lead me hither into temptation. I confess I might think indeed it was a kind of honorable challenge, to meet privately,  15
without seconds, and decide the difference betwixt the two sexes; but heaven forgive me if I thought amiss.

DORALICE.

You thought too, I'll lay my life on't, that you might as well make love to me, as my husband does to your mistress.  20

PALAMEDE.

I was so unreasonable to think so too.

DORALICE.

And then you wickedly inferred that there was some justice in the revenge of it, or at least but little injury, for a man to endeavor to enjoy that which he accounts a blessing and which is not valued as it ought by the dull  25
possessor. Confess your wickedness, did you not think so?

PALAMEDE.

I confess I was thinking so, as fast as I could; but you think so much before me, that you will let me think nothing.  30

DORALICE.

'Tis the very thing I designed: I have forestalled all your arguments, and left you without a word more to plead for mercy. If you have anything farther to offer ere sen-
tence pass— Poor animal, I brought you hither only for my diversion.  35

PALAMEDE.

That you may have, if you'll make use of me the right

26. your] *Q1–2, Q4, C1–2;* you *Q3.*     *Q3–4.*
34. animal,] *Q1–2, C1–2;* animal!

---

9. *to*] as to.

way; but I tell thee, woman, I am now past talking.

DORALICE.

But it may be I came hither to hear what fine things you
could say for yourself.

PALAMEDE.

You would be very angry, to my knowledge, if I should 40
lose so much time to say many of 'em— By this hand you
would—

DORALICE.

Fie, Palamede, I am a woman of honor.

PALAMEDE.

I see you are; you have kept touch with your assignation;
and before we part, you shall find that I am a man of 45
honor. —Yet I have one scruple of conscience—

DORALICE.

I warrant you will not want some naughty argument or
other to satisfy yourself. I hope you are afraid of betraying your friend?

PALAMEDE.

Of betraying my friend! I am more afraid of being be- 50
trayed by you to my friend. You women now are got into
the way of telling first yourselves: a man who has any
care of his reputation will be loath to trust it with you.

DORALICE.

O, you charge your faults upon our sex. You men are
like cocks; you never make love but you clap your wings 55
and crow when you have done.

PALAMEDE.

Nay, rather you women are like hens; you never lay but
you cackle an hour after, to discover your nest. —But I'll
venture it for once.

DORALICE.

To convince you that you are in the wrong, I'll retire into 60
the dark grotto to my devotion, and make so little noise
that it shall be impossible for you to find me.

PALAMEDE.

But if I find you—

---

54. your] *Q1–3, C1–2;* you *Q4.*

58. *discover*] reveal.

DORALICE.

Ay, if you find me—but I'll put you to search in more
corners than you imagine.                                         65

*She runs in, and he after her.*

*Enter* Rhodophil *and* Melantha.

MELANTHA.

Let me die, but this solitude, and that grotto, are scan-
dalous; I'll go no further. Besides, you have a sweet lady
of your own.

RHODOPHIL.

But a sweet mistress, now and then, makes my sweet lady
so much more sweet.                                              70

MELANTHA.

I hope you will not force me?

RHODOPHIL.

But I will, if you desire it.

PALAMEDE (*within*).

Where the devil are you, madam? S'death, I begin to be
weary of this hide and seek. If you stay a little longer, till
the fit's over, I'll hide in my turn, and put you to the     75
finding me.

*He enters, and sees* Rhodophil *and* Melantha.

How! Rhodophil and my mistress!

MELANTHA [*aside*].

My servant to apprehend me! This is *surprenant au dernier*.

RHODOPHIL [*aside*].

I must on; there's nothing but impudence can help me     80
out.

PALAMEDE.

Rhodophil, how came you hither in so good company?

---

67. further] *Q1–4, C2;* farther *C1.*      78. *surprenant*] *Q1–2, C1–2;* sup-
76. me] *Q1–2, C1–2;* of me *Q3–4.*        renant *Q3–4.*

65.1. S.D. *in*] i.e., to the inner stage behind the proscenium.
73. *S'death*] a milder form of the oath, "God's death."
78–79. *surprenant au dernier*] astonishing to the utmost.

RHODOPHIL.

As you see, Palamede, an effect of pure friendship; I was
not able to live without you.

PALAMEDE.

But what makes my mistress with you?                          85

RHODOPHIL.

Why, I heard you were here alone, and could not in
civility but bring her to you.

MELANTHA.

You'll pardon the effects of a passion which I may now
avow for you, if it transported me beyond the rules of
*bienséance*.                                                 90

PALAMEDE.

But who told you I was here? They that told you that,
may tell you more, for aught I know.

RHODOPHIL.

O, for that matter, we had intelligence.

PALAMEDE.

But let me tell you, we came hither so very privately that
you could not trace us.                                       95

RHODOPHIL.

Us? What us? You are alone.

PALAMEDE.

Us! The devil's in me for mistaking: me, I meant. Or us;
that is, you are me, or I you, as we are friends: that's us.

DORALICE (*within*).

Palamede, Palamede.

RHODOPHIL.

I should know that voice: who's within there that calls 100
you?

PALAMEDE.

Faith, I can't imagine; I believe the place is haunted.

---

86. Why,] *Q1, Q3–4, C1–2;* Why
*Q2.*
94. so very] *Q1–3, C1–2;* so *Q4.*
97. me, I] *Q1–3, C1–2;* I *Q4.*
100. voice:] *this edn.;* voice? *Q1–4,*

*C1–2.*
100. there] *Q1, Q3–4, C1–2;* their
*Q2.*
102. the] *Q1–3, C1–2;* that *Q4.*

90. *bienséance*] propriety, decorum.
91–92. *They . . . know*] possibly an aside (Sutherland, p. 146).

DORALICE (*within*).

Palamede, Palamede, all cocks hidden.

PALAMEDE.

> Lord, lord, what shall I do? —Well, dear friend, to let
> you see I scorn to be jealous, and that I dare trust my 105
> mistress with you, take her back, for I would not willingly
> have her frighted, and I am resolved to see who's there.
> I'll not be daunted with a bugbear, that's certain. Prithee,
> dispute it not, it shall be so; nay, do not put me to swear,
> but go quickly: there's an effect of pure friendship for 110
> you now.

> *Enter* Doralice, *and looks amazed, seeing them*.

RHODOPHIL.

> Doralice! I am thunderstruck to see you here.

PALAMEDE.

> So am I! quite thunderstruck. Was it you that called me
> within? —(*Aside*.)   I must be impudent.

RHODOPHIL.

> How came you hither, spouse?                                     115

PALAMEDE.

> Ay, how came you hither? And, which is more, how
> could you be here without my knowledge?

DORALICE (*to her husband*).

> O, gentleman, have I caught you i'faith? have I broke
> forth in ambush upon you? I thought my suspicions
> would prove true.                                               120

RHODOPHIL.

> Suspicions! this is very fine, spouse! Prithee what sus-
> picions?

DORALICE.

> O, you feign ignorance. Why, of you and Melantha.
> Here I have stayed these two hours, waiting with all the

110–111. for you now] *Q1–2, C2;*   121. spouse! Prithee] *C2;* spouse!/
for you *Q3–4;* now *C1.*              Prithee *(printed as verse) Q1–4, C1.*
118–119. i'faith? . . . you?] *Works;*   124. these] *Q1–3, C1–2;* this *Q4.*
i'faith! . . . you! *Q1–4, C1–2.*

   103. *all cocks hidden*] "Possibly a cry in a children's game, as in hide-
and-go-seek (see V. 318); Sutherland thinks it may refer to the practice of
covering up the cocks just before releasing them for a fight" (B-B, p. 326).
The bawdry aside, Doralice is ready for Palamede to come to her.

rage of a passionate, loving wife, but infinitely jealous, to 125
take you two in the manner; for hither I was certain you
would come.

RHODOPHIL.

But you are mistaken, spouse, in the occasion; for we
came hither on purpose to find Palamede, on intelligence he was gone before.                                    130

PALAMEDE.

I'll be hanged then if the same party who gave you intelligence I was here did not tell your wife you would come
hither: now I smell malice on't on both sides.

DORALICE.

Was it so, think you? nay, then, I'll confess my part of the
malice too. As soon as ever I spied my husband and 135
Melantha come together, I had a strange temptation to
make him jealous in revenge; and that made me call
"Palamede, Palamede," as though there had been an intrigue between us.

MELANTHA.

Nay, I avow there was an appearance of an intrigue be- 140
tween us too.

PALAMEDE.

To see how things will come about!

RHODOPHIL.

And was it only thus, my dear Doralice?        *Embraces [her].*

DORALICE.

And did I wrong none, Rhodophil, with a false suspicion?
                                               *Embracing him.*

PALAMEDE (*aside*).

Now am I confident we had all four the same design. 'Tis 145
a pretty odd kind of game this, where each of us plays for
double stakes: this is just thrust and parry with the same
motion; I am to get his wife, and yet to guard my own

---

129. hither on] *Q1–3, C1–2;* hither
on the *Q4.*
140. avow] *Q1, C1–2;* vow *Q2–4.*

144. none] *Q1–4, C1;* n'own *C2.*
145. am I] *Q1–3, C1–2;* I am *Q4.*

---

126. *in the manner*] *in flagrante delicto*, in a sinful act. Cf. John Day, *The Isle of Gulls* (1606): "I ran to Manasses, thinking to take my husband and his wife in the manner" (cited in Tilley).

144. *none*] Summers, 3:547, notes that this expression is a contraction of "mine own" by way of "myn own" and hence "none"; baby talk.

mistress. But I am vilely suspicious that while I conquer
in the right wing, I shall be routed in the left. For both  150
our women will certainly betray their party, because they
are each of them for gaining of two, as well as we; and I
much fear,

      If their necessities and ours were known,
      They have more need of two, than we of one.    155
                   *Exeunt, embracing one another.*

155.1. *one another*] *Q1, C1–2; each
other Q2–4.*

# ACT IV

[IV.i]   *Enter* Leonidas, *musing,* Amalthea *following him.*

AMALTHEA.

Yonder he is, and I must speak or die;
And yet 'tis death to speak; yet he must know
I have a passion for him, and may know it
With a less blush, because to offer it
To his low fortunes shows I loved before          5
His person, not his greatness.

LEONIDAS.

First scorned, and now commanded from the court!
The king is good, but he is wrought to this
By proud Argaleon's malice.
What more disgrace can love and fortune join         10
T'inflict upon one man? I cannot now
Behold my dear Palmyra: she perhaps too
Is grown ashamed of a mean ill-placed love.

AMALTHEA *(aside).*

Assist me, Venus, for I tremble when
I am to speak, but I must force myself.          15
*(To him.)* Sir, I would crave but one short minute with you,
And some few words.

LEONIDAS *(aside).*          The proud Argaleon's sister!

AMALTHEA *(aside).*

Alas, it will not out; shame stops my mouth.
[*To him.*]   Pardon my error, sir, I was mistaken,
And took you for another.          20

LEONIDAS *(aside).*

In spite of all his guards, I'll see Palmyra;
Though meanly born, I have a kingly soul yet.

AMALTHEA *(aside).*

I stand upon a precipice where fain
I would retire, but love still thrusts me on.

---

11. one] *Q1, Q3–4, C1–2;* on *Q2.*

---

2. *'tis death to speak*] Perhaps Leonidas's exile from court carries
with it an order forbidding any communication.

    Now I grow bolder, and will speak to him.        25
    *(To him.)*   Sir, 'tis indeed to you that I would speak,
    And if—
LEONIDAS.    O, you are sent to scorn my fortunes;
    Your sex and beauty are your privilege;
    But should your brother—
AMALTHEA [*aside*].
    Now he looks angry, and I dare not speak.       30
    [*To him.*]  I had some business with you, sir,
    But 'tis not worth your knowledge.
LEONIDAS.
    Then 'twill be charity to let me mourn
    My griefs alone, for I am much disordered.
AMALTHEA.
    'Twill be more charity to mourn 'em with you:    35
    Heav'n knows I pity you.
LEONIDAS.              Your pity, madam,
    Is generous, but 'tis unavailable.
AMALTHEA.
    You know not till 'tis tried.
    Your sorrows are no secret; you have lost
    A crown, and mistress.
LEONIDAS.          Are not these enough?    40
    Hang two such weights on any other soul,
    And see if it can bear 'em.
AMALTHEA.
    More; you are banished, by my brother's means,
    And ne'er must hope again to see your princess,
    Except as pris'ners view fair walks and streets    45
    And careless passengers going by their grates,
    To make 'em feel the want of liberty.
    But, worse than all,
    The king this morning has enjoined his daughter

---

34. griefs] *Q1–4, C2;* grief's *C1.*

---

    37. *unavailable*] unavailing.
    41–42. *Hang . . . bear 'em*] "The image . . . is drawn from the familiar emblem of the growing palm tree weighed down on either side with two stones to make it grow straight" (*Works,* 11:500).
    46. *careless . . . grates*] carefree passersby going past their prison bars.

T'accept my brother's love.
LEONIDAS.                    Is this your pity?                    50
    You aggravate my griefs and print 'em deeper
    In new and heavier stamps.
AMALTHEA.
    'Tis as physicians show the desperate ill
    T'endear their art, by mitigating pains
    They cannot wholly cure: when you despair                    55
    Of all you wish, some part of it, because
    Unhoped for, may be grateful; and some other—
LEONIDAS.
    What other?
AMALTHEA.
    Some other may—
    (Aside.)    My shame again has seized me, and I can go    60
    No farther—
LEONIDAS.
    These often failings, sighs, and interruptions
    Make me imagine you have grief like mine:
    Have you ne'er loved?
AMALTHEA.                    I? never. —(Aside).    'Tis in vain,
    I must despair in silence.                    65
LEONIDAS.
    You come as I suspected, then, to mock,
    At least observe, my griefs: take it not ill
    That I must leave you.                    ⌐Is going.
AMALTHEA.
    You must not go with these unjust opinions.
    Command my life and fortunes; you are wise,                    70
    Think, and think well, what I can do to serve you.
LEONIDAS.
    I have but one thing in my thoughts and wishes:
    If by your means I can obtain the sight
    Of my adored Palmyra, or, what's harder,
    One minute's time, to tell her I die hers—                    75

56. you] *Q1–3, C1–2;* your *Q4.*          64. I?] *Q1–2, C1–2;* I! *Q3–4.*
62. failings,] *Q3–4, Works;* failing,          66. come] *Q1, C1–2;* came *Q2–4.*
*Q1–2;* failing *C1–2, Sutherland, B-B.*

62. *often failings*] frequent reductions of vocal volume.

*She starts back.*

I see I am not to expect it from you,
Nor could, indeed, with reason.

AMALTHEA.

Name any other thing: is Amalthea
So despicable, she can serve your wishes
In this alone?

LEONIDAS.      If I should ask of heav'n,      80
I have no other suit.

AMALTHEA.

To show you, then, I can deny you nothing,
Though 'tis more hard to me than any other,
Yet I will do't for you.

LEONIDAS.

Name quickly, name the means; speak, my good angel.    85

AMALTHEA.

Be not so much o'erjoyed; for, if you are,
I'll rather die than do't. This night the court
Will be in masquerade.
You shall attend on me; in that disguise
You may both see and speak to her,      90
If you dare venture it.

LEONIDAS.

Yes, were a god her guardian,
And bore in each hand thunder, I would venture.

AMALTHEA.

Farewell then; two hours hence I will expect you.
[*Aside.*]    My heart's so full that I can stay no longer.      95
                            *Exit.*

LEONIDAS.

Already it grows dusky; I'll prepare
With haste for my disguise. But who are these?

*Enter* Hermogenes *and* Eubulus.

HERMOGENES.

'Tis he; we need not fear to speak to him.

EUBULUS.

Leonidas.

LEONIDAS.      Sure I have known that voice.

HERMOGENES.

    You have some reason, sir; 'tis Eubulus,                    100
    Who bred you with the princess, and departing
    Bequeathed you to my care.

LEONIDAS *(kneeling)*.

    My foster-father! let my knees express
    My joys for your return!

EUBULUS.

    Rise, sir, you must not kneel.

LEONIDAS.                    E'er since you left me,           105
    I have been wand'ring in a maze of fate,
    Led by false fires of a fantastic glory
    And the vain luster of imagined crowns.
    But ah! why would you leave me? or how could you
    Absent yourself so long?                                          110

EUBULUS.

    I'll give you a most just account of both:
    And something more I have to tell you which
    I know must cause your wonder; but this place,
    Though almost hid in darkness, is not safe.
    Already I discern some coming toward us                           115
                              *Torches appear.*
    With lights who may discover me. Hermogenes,
    Your lodgings are hard by and much more private.

HERMOGENES.

    There you may freely speak.

LEONIDAS.                 Let us make haste,
    For some affairs and of no small importance
    Call me another way.             *Exeunt.*                 120

*Enter* Palamede *and* Rhodophil, *with vizor-masks in their hands and torches before 'em.*

PALAMEDE.

    We shall have noble sport tonight, Rhodophil; this mas-
querading is a most glorious invention.

---

101. bred] *Q1, Q4, C1–2;* bread    113. know] *Q1–2,   C1–2;*   now
*Q2–3.*                             *Q3–4.*

    120.2. *torches*] men or boys bearing torches.

RHODOPHIL.

I believe it was invented first by some jealous lover to discover the haunts of his jilting mistress, or perhaps by some distressed servant to gain an opportunity with a 125 jealous man's wife.

PALAMEDE.

No, it must be the invention of a woman: it has so much of subtlety and love in it.

RHODOPHIL.

I am sure 'tis extremely pleasant, for to go unknown is the next degree to going invisible.                    130

PALAMEDE.

What with our antique habits and feigned voices—do you know me? and I know you?—methinks we move and talk just like so many overgrown puppets.

RHODOPHIL.

Masquerade is only vizor-mask improved, a heightening of the same fashion.                    135

PALAMEDE.

No, masquerade is vizor-mask in debauch, and I like it the better for't: for with a vizor-mask we fool ourselves into courtship for the sake of an eye that glanced or a hand that stole itself out of a glove sometimes to give us a sample of the skin. But in masquerade there is nothing 140 to be known; she's all *terra incognita* and the bold discoverer leaps ashore and takes his lot among the wild Indians and savages without the vile consideration of safety to his person or of beauty or wholesomeness in his mistress.                    145

*Enter* Beliza.

RHODOPHIL.

Beliza, what make you here?

BELIZA.

Sir, my lady sent me after you to let you know she finds

130. going] *Q1–2, C1–2; go Q3–4.*
131. with] *Q1–3, C1–2;* without
*Q4.*

131. *antique*] "used either in the sense of 'ancient' or 'antic' " (*Works*, 11:500).

herself a little indisposed, so that she cannot be at court
but is retired to rest in her own apartment where she
shall want the happiness of your dear embraces tonight. 150

RHODOPHIL.

A very fine phrase, Beliza, to let me know my wife de-
sires to lie alone.

PALAMEDE.

I doubt, Rhodophil, you take the pains sometimes to
instruct your wife's woman in these elegancies.

RHODOPHIL.

Tell my dear lady that since I must be so unhappy as not 155
to wait on her tonight, I will lament bitterly for her absence. 'Tis true, I shall be at court, but I will take no
divertissement there; and when I return to my solitary
bed, if I am so forgetful of my passion as to sleep, I will
dream of her, and betwixt sleep and waking put out my 160
foot toward her side for midnight consolation, and not
finding her, I will sigh and imagine myself a most deso-
late widower.

BELIZA.

I shall do your commands, sir.                         *Exit.*

RHODOPHIL *(aside).*

She's sick as aptly for my purpose as if she had contrived 165
it so. Well, if ever woman was a helpmate for man, my
spouse is so; for within this hour I received a note from
Melantha that she would meet me this evening in masquerade in boy's habit to rejoice with me before she en-
tered into fetters, for I find she loves me better than 170
Palamede only because he's to be her husband. There's
something of antipathy in the word "marriage" to the
nature of love; marriage is the mere ladle of affection
that cools it when 'tis never so fiercely boiling over.

PALAMEDE.

Dear Rhodophil, I must needs beg your pardon: there is 175

---

154. woman ]*Q1–3, C1–2;* women    166. for man] *Q1–3, C1–2;* for a
*Q4.*                                man *Q4.*
166. was a] *Q1–4, C2;* was *C1.*

---

150. *want*] lack.
153. *doubt*] suspect.

an occasion fallen out which I had forgot; I cannot be at court tonight.

RHODOPHIL.

Dear Palamede, I am sorry we shall not have one course together at the herd; but I find your game lies single: good fortune to you with your mistress.      *Exit.* 180

PALAMEDE.

He has wished me good fortune with his wife: there's no sin in this then, there's fair leave given. Well, I must go visit the sick; I cannot resist the temptations of my charity. O what a difference will she find betwixt a dull resty husband and a quick vigorous lover! he sets out like a 185 carrier's horse, plodding on because he knows he must, with the bells of matrimony chiming so melancholy about his neck, in pain till he's at his journey's end; and despairing to get thither, he is fain to fortify imagination with the thoughts of another woman. I take heat after 190 heat like a well-breathed courser and— *(Clashing of swords within.)*   But hark, what noise is that? swords! Nay, then, have with you.      *Exit* Palamede.

*Re-enter* Palamede, *with* Rhodophil, *and* Doralice *in man's habit.*

RHODOPHIL.

Friend, your relief was very timely, otherwise I had been oppressed.                                                   195

PALAMEDE.

What was the quarrel?

RHODOPHIL.

What I did was in rescue of this youth.

PALAMEDE.

What cause could he give 'em?

DORALICE.

The cause was nothing but only the common cause of fighting in masquerades: they were drunk and I was 200 sober.

187. with the] *Q1–4, C2;* with he      190. the] *Q1–4, C2;* the the *C1*
*C1.*

178–179. *course . . . herd*] "an analogy to hunting, coursing game, probably deer, with hounds" (B-B, p. 333).
184. *resty*] sluggish, indolent (*OED* cites this passage).

RHODOPHIL.

Have they not hurt you?

DORALICE.

No, but I am exceeding ill with the fright on't.

PALAMEDE.

Let's lead him to some place where he may refresh him-
self.                                                                                     205

RHODOPHIL.

Do you conduct him then.

PALAMEDE *(aside)*.

How cross this happens to my design of going to Doralice! for I am confident she was sick on purpose that I
should visit her. —Hark you, Rhodophil, could not you
take care of the stripling? I am partly engaged tonight. 210

RHODOPHIL.

You know I have business; but come, youth, if it must be
so.

DORALICE *(to* Rhodophil).

No, good sir, do not give yourself that trouble; I shall be
safer and better pleased with your friend here.

RHODOPHIL.

Farewell then; once more I wish you a good adventure. 215

PALAMEDE [*aside*].

Damn this kindness! now must I be troubled with this
young rogue and miss my opportunity with Doralice.

*Exeunt,* Rhodophil *alone,* Palamede *with* Doralice.

[IV.ii]                          *Enter* Polydamas.

[POLYDAMAS.]

Argaleon counseled well to banish him;
He has, I know not what,
Of greatness in his looks and of high fate
That almost awes me; but I fear my daughter,
Who hourly moves me for him, and I marked                    5
She sighed when I but named Argaleon to her.

210. the] *Q1–3, C1–2;* this *Q4.*          2. what,] *Q1–3, C1–2;* what *Q4.*
217.1. *Exeunt,] this edn.; Exit Q1–4,*     3. of high] *Q1–3, C1–2;* high of
*C1–2.*                                      *Q4.*

But see, the maskers: hence, my cares, this night;
At least take truce and find me on my pillow.

*Enter the* Princess, *in masquerade, with ladies. At the other end,* Argaleon *and gentlemen in masquerade; then* Leonidas *leading* Amalthea.
*The* King *sits. A dance. After the dance:*

AMALTHEA *(to* Leonidas).
    That's the princess;
    I saw the habit ere she put it on.                           10
LEONIDAS.
    I know her by a thousand other signs:
    She cannot hide so much divinity.
    Disguised, and silent, yet some graceful motion
    Breaks from her and shines round her like a glory.
                                          *Goes to* Palmyra.
AMALTHEA.
    Thus she reveals herself and knows it not.                   15
    Like love's dark lantern I direct his steps
    And yet he sees not that which gives him light.
PALMYRA *(to* Leonidas).
    I know you; but alas, Leonidas,
    Why should you tempt this danger on yourself?
LEONIDAS.
    Madam, you know me not if you believe                        20
    I would not hazard greater for your sake.
    But you I fear are changed.
PALMYRA.
    No, I am still the same.
    But there are many things became Palmyra
    Which ill become the princess.
LEONIDAS.                            I ask nothing               25
    Which honor will not give you leave to grant:
    One hour's short audience, at my father's house,
    You cannot sure refuse me.
PALMYRA.
    Perhaps I should, did I consult strict virtue;
    But something must be given to love and you.                 30
    When would you I should come?

19. this] *Q1–3, C1–2;* the *Q4.*

LEONIDAS.

   This evening with the speediest opportunity.
   I have a secret to discover to you
   Which will surprise and please you.

PALMYRA.                    'Tis enough.

   Go now, for we may be observed and known.      35
   I trust your honor; give me not occasion
   To blame myself or you.

LEONIDAS.

   You never shall repent your good opinion.

                     *Kisses her hand, and exit.*

ARGALEON.

   I cannot be deceived; that is the princess.
   One of her maids betrayed the habit to me;      40
   But who was he with whom she held discourse?
   'Tis one she favors, for he kissed her hand.
   Our shapes are like, our habits near the same;
   She may mistake and speak to me for him.
   I am resolved I'll satisfy my doubts          45
   Though to be more tormented.        *Exit.*

SONG

1

Whilst Alexis lay pressed
In her arms he loved best,
With his hands round her neck,
And his head on her breast,             50
He found the fierce pleasure too hasty to stay,
And his soul in the tempest just flying away.

2

When Cælia saw this,
With a sigh and a kiss
She cried, "O my dear, I am robbed of my bliss;   55
'Tis unkind to your love and unfaithfully done
To leave me behind you and die all alone."

---

   47–67. *Song*] See *Works*, 11:501, for the French source of this song,
and 11:608–609, for textual variants in other printings.
   57. *die*] experience sexual climax.

3

The youth, though in haste
And breathing his last,
In pity died slowly while she died more fast;            60
Till at length she cried, "Now, my dear, now let us go,
Now die, my Alexis, and I will die too."

4

Thus entranced they did lie
Till Alexis did try
To recover new breath that again he might die.          65
Then often they died; but the more they did so,
The nymph died more quick and the shepherd more slow.

*Another dance. After it,* Argaleon *re-enters and stands by the*
Princess.

PALMYRA *(to* Argaleon).

    Leonidas, what means this quick return?
ARGALEON [*aside*].

    O heav'n! 'tis what I feared.
PALMYRA.

    Is aught of moment happened since you went?      70
ARGALEON.

    No madam, but I understood not fully
    Your last commands.
PALMYRA.                              And yet you answered to 'em.

    Retire; you are too indiscreet a lover.
    I'll meet you where I promised.                *Exit.*
ARGALEON.

    O my cursed fortune! what have I discovered?     75
    But I will be revenged.          *Whispers to the King.*
POLYDAMAS.

    But are you certain you are not deceived?
ARGALEON.

    Upon my life.
POLYDAMAS.        Her honor is concerned.

68. S.P. *to* Argaleon] *Q1–3, C1–2;*
*om. Q4.*
77. are you] *Q1–4, C2;* are yon *C1.*

Somewhat I'll do, but I am yet distracted
And know not where to fix. I wished a child          80
And heav'n, in anger, granted my request.
So blind we are, our wishes are so vain,
That what we most desire proves most our pain.

*Exeunt omnes.*

[IV.iii]

*An eating house. Bottles of wine on the table.* Palamede, *and* Doralice *in man's habit.*

DORALICE *(aside).*

Now cannot I find in my heart to discover myself,
though I long he should know me.

PALAMEDE.

I tell thee, boy, now I have seen thee safe I must be gone.
I have no leisure to throw away on thy raw conversation:
I am a person that understand better things, I.          5

DORALICE.

Were I a woman, O how you'd admire me! cry up every
word I said, and screw your face into a submissive smile,
as I have seen a dull gallant act wit and counterfeit pleas-
antness when he whispers to a great person in a playhouse, smile and look briskly when the other answers, as   10
if something of extraordinary had passed betwixt 'em
when, heaven knows, there was nothing else but "What a
clock does your lordship think it is?" and my lord's *repartie* is " 'Tis almost parktime," or at most, "Shall we out of
the pit and go behind the scenes for an act or two?" And   15
yet such fine things as these would be wit in a mistress's
mouth.

PALAMEDE.

Ay, boy, there's dame Nature in the case: he who cannot
find wit in a mistress deserves to find nothing else, boy.
But these are riddles to thee, child, and I have not leisure   20

5. understand] *Q1–4, C1, Suther-*      *Q3.*
*land, B-B;* understands *C2, Works.*      20. not] *Q1–4, C2;* no *C1.*
13. think] *Q1–2, Q4, C1–2;* thing

14. *parktime*] i.e., the fashionable time to go to the park.

to instruct thee; I have affairs to dispatch, great affairs; I
am a man of business.

DORALICE.

Come, you shall not go. You have no affairs but what you
may dispatch here, to my knowledge.

PALAMEDE.

I find now thou art a boy of more understanding than I    25
thought thee, a very lewd wicked boy. O' my conscience
thou wouldst debauch me, and hast some evil design
upon my person.

DORALICE.

You are mistaken, sir; I would only have you show me a
more lawful reason why you would leave me, than I can    30
why you should not, and I'll not stay you. For I am not so
young but I understand the necessities of flesh and
blood and the pressing occasions of mankind as well as
you.

PALAMEDE.

A very forward and understanding boy! Thou art in        35
great danger of a page's wit, to be brisk at fourteen and
dull at twenty. But I'll give thee no further account; I
must and will go.

DORALICE.

My life on't, your mistress is not at home.

PALAMEDE [*aside*].

This imp will make me very angry. —I tell thee, young    40
sir, she is at home; and at home for me; and which is
more, she is abed for me, and sick for me.

DORALICE.

For you only?

PALAMEDE.

Ay, for me only.

---

27. hast] *Q1–2, C1–2;* has *Q3–4.*          *Q3–4, C1.*
36–37. fourteen . . . twenty] *Q3–4,*        43. only?] *Q1–2, Q4, C1–2;* only.
*C2;* 14 . . . 20 *Q1–2, C1.*                *Q3.*
37. further] *Q1–2, C2;* farther

24. *dispatch here*] *Works,* 11:501, notes that eating houses were favorite locations for sexual intrigue.
30. *lawful*] permissible; allowable; justifiable (*OED*).

DORALICE.

But how do you know she's sick abed? 45

PALAMEDE.

She sent her husband word so.

DORALICE.

And are you such a novice in love to believe a wife's message to her husband?

PALAMEDE.

Why, what the devil should be her meaning else?

DORALICE.

It may be to go in masquerade as well as you, to observe 50 your haunts and keep you company without your knowledge.

PALAMEDE.

Nay, I'll trust her for that: she loves me too well to disguise herself from me.

DORALICE.

If I were she, I would disguise on purpose to try your wit 55 and come to my servant like a riddle—read me and take me.

PALAMEDE.

I would know her in any shape: my good genius would prompt me to find out a handsome woman. There's something in her that would attract me to her without 60 my knowledge.

DORALICE.

Then you make a lodestone of your mistress?

PALAMEDE.

Yes, and I carry steel about me which has been so often touched that it never fails to point to the north pole.

---

63. steel] *Q1–3, C1–2;* a steel *Q4.*

---

56–57. *read . . . me*]"Probably a formula from printed riddles, with a pun on 'ride me, and take me' " (B-B, p. 338).

58. *genius*] attendant spirit, intuition personified.

62–64. *lodestone . . . pole*] "The meaning is sexual as well as scientific" (*Works,* 11:50). (There may be additional nuance intended in the original spelling of "load-stone.") Steel placed in a magnetic field (as when a magnet is rubbed along a nail) retains magnetism for some time even when the source of the field is removed. See below, IV.iii.81–83.

DORALICE.

Yet still my mind gives me that you have met her dis-    65
guised tonight and have not known her.

PALAMEDE [*aside*].

This is the most pragmatical conceited little fellow; he
will needs understand my business better than myself.
—I tell thee once more, thou dost not know my mistress.

DORALICE.

And I tell you once more that I know her better than you    70
do.

PALAMEDE [*aside*].

The boy's resolved to have the last word. I find I must go
without reply.                                              *Exit.*

DORALICE.

Ah mischief, I have lost him with my fooling. Palamede,
Palamede.                                                   75

*He returns. She plucks off her peruke and puts it on again when he knows
her.*

PALAMEDE.

O heavens! Is it you, madam?

DORALICE.

Now, where was your good genius that would prompt
you to find me out?

PALAMEDE.

Why, you see I was not deceived; you yourself were my
good genius.                                               80

DORALICE.

But where was the steel, that knew the lodestone? ha?

PALAMEDE.

The truth is, madam, the steel has lost its virtue, and
therefore, if you please, we'll new touch it.

*Enter* Rhodophil, *and* Melantha *in boy's habit.* Rhodophil *sees* Palamede *kissing Doralice's hand.*

---

69. thee] *Q1–3, C1–2;* the *Q4.*          81. ha?] *Q1–2, C1–2;* ha! *Q3–4.*
72. boy's] *Q1–3, C1–2;* boy is *Q4.*      82. has] *Q1–2, C1–2;* hath *Q3–4.*

67. *pragmatical*] officious, meddlesome, interfering, intrusive
(*OED*).

RHODOPHIL.

Palamede again! Am I fallen into your quarters? What?
Engaging with a boy? Is all honorable?                    85

PALAMEDE.

O, very honorable on my side. I was just chastising this
young villain; he was running away without paying his
share of the reckoning.

RHODOPHIL.

Then I find I was deceived in him.

PALAMEDE.

Yes, you are deceived in him: 'tis the archest rogue if you   90
did but know him.

MELANTHA [to Rhodophil].

Good Rhodophil, let us get off à la dérobé for fear I
should be discovered.

RHODOPHIL [to Melantha].

There's no retiring now; I warrant you for discovery.
Now have I the oddest thought, to entertain you before   95
your servant's face, and he never the wiser; 'twill be the
prettiest juggling trick to cheat him when he looks upon
us.

MELANTHA [to him].

This is the strangest caprice in you.

PALAMEDE (to Doralice).

This Rhodophil's the unluckest fellow to me! This is now  100
the second time he has barred the dice when we were just
ready to have nicked him; but if ever I get the box
again—

DORALICE [to Palamede].

Do you think he will not know me? Am I like myself?

---

85. boy?] Q1–2, C1–2; boy, Q3–4.        92. à la dérobé]e al-a derobbée Q1–4,
90. you are] Q1–2, Q4, C1–2; your        C1–2 (al-a-derobbée Q3–4).
are Q3.

---

92. à la dérobé] clandestinely, by stealth, "on the sly."
94. warrant . . . discovery] guarantee you won't be discovered.
101–102. barred . . . box] To bar the dice is to declare a cast void; to
nick another player is to win over him. The person who casts the dice and
so directs the game shakes the dice in a box and throws them out of it.

PALAMEDE [*to her*].

No more than a picture in the hangings.                    105

DORALICE [*to him*].

Nay, then he can never discover me now the wrong side
of the arras is turned toward him.

PALAMEDE [*to her*].

At least 'twill be some pleasure to me to enjoy what freedom I can while he looks on; I will storm the outworks of
matrimony even before his face.                            110

RHODOPHIL.

What wine have you there, Palamede?

PALAMEDE.

Old Chios, or the rogue's damned that drew it.

RHODOPHIL.

Come, to the most constant of mistresses: that, I believe,
is yours, Palamede.

DORALICE.

Pray spare your seconds; for my part, I am but a weak     115
brother.

PALAMEDE.

Now, to the truest of turtles: that is, your wife, Rhodophil, that lies sick at home in the bed of honor.

RHODOPHIL.

Now, let's have one common health, and so have done.

DORALICE.

Then for once I'll begin it. Here's to him that has the    120
fairest lady of Sicily in masquerade tonight.

PALAMEDE.

This is such an obliging health, I'll kiss thee, dear rogue,
for thy invention.                              *Kisses her.*

---

105. *hangings*] woven tapestries depicting scenes and figures.

106–107. *wrong side of the arras*]An arras or tapestry is designed with
one finished side only; the figures and scenes on the unfinished side
would be considerably less distinct.

109. *outworks*] minor defensive positions constructed outside the
main defense perimeter.

112. *Old Chios*] wine of the Greek isle of Chios. A heavy, sweet, dark
red wine, frequently cut with water (information supplied by Mr. George
Korman).

115–116. *seconds . . . weak brother*] joiners in the toast; "I am a poor
drinker."

117. *turtles*] turtledoves, lovers.

RHODOPHIL.

He who has this lady is a happy man, without dispute.
—(*Aside.*) I'm most concerned in this, I am sure.          125

PALAMEDE.

Was it not well found out, Rhodophil?

MELANTHA.

Ay, this was *bien trouvé* indeed.

DORALICE (*to* Melantha).

I suppose I shall do you a kindness to inquire if you have
not been in France, sir?

MELANTHA.

To do you service, sir.                                     130

DORALICE.

O, *monsieur, votre valet bien humble.*          *Saluting her.*

MELANTHA.

*Votre escalve, monsieur, de tout mon coeur.*

*Returning the salute.*

DORALICE.

I suppose, sweet sir, you are the hope and joy of some
thriving citizen who has pinched himself at home to
breed you abroad, where you have learnt your exercises, 135
as it appears, most awkwardly, and are returned with the
addition of a new-laced bosom and a clap to your good
old father, who looks at you with his mouth while you
spout French with your man *monsieur.*

PALAMEDE.

Let me kiss thee again for that, dear rogue.                140

---

130. sir.] *Q1–4, C2*; sir? *C1*.
131. *votre*] *C2; vot Q1–4. C1*.
132. *Votre*] *this edn.; Votre Q1–4,
C1; Votré C2*.
139. man  *monsieur*] *Q1–3,  C1–2*

(*Man Monsieur*), Sutherland (man
monsieur); *Mon Monsieur Q4, B-B,
Works.*
140. thee] *Q1–3, C1–2*; the *Q4*.

---

126. *found out*] devised, invented (*OED*)—i.e., the toast.
127. *bien trouvé*] felicitous, original.
131. S.D. *Saluting*] kissing.
137. *clap*] case of gonorrhea.
138. *with his mouth*] openmouthed.
139. *man* monsieur] French valet (Sutherland, p. 147). (A disputed
reading. B-B, p. 148, and *Works*, 11:502, argue for "*mon monsieur*," i.e.,
that he addresses his father condescendingly as "my good man.")

MELANTHA.

And you, I imagine, are my young master whom your
mother durst not trust upon salt water, but left you to be
your own tutor at fourteen, to be very brisk and *entrepre-
nant,* to endeavor to be debauched ere you have learnt
the knack on't, to value yourself upon a clap before you  145
can get it, and to make it the height of your ambition to
get a player for your mistress.

RHODOPHIL (*embracing* Melantha).

O dear young bully, thou hast tickled him with a *repartie,*
i'faith.

MELANTHA.

You are one of those that applaud our country plays  150
where drums and trumpets and blood and wounds are
wit.

RHODOPHIL.

Again, my boy? Let me kiss thee most abundantly.

DORALICE.

You are an admirer of the dull French poetry, which is
so thin that it is the very leaf-gold of wit, the very wafers  155
and whipped cream of sense, for which a man opens his
mouth and gapes to swallow nothing; and to be an admirer of such profound dullness, one must be endowed
with a great perfection of impudence and ignorance.

PALAMEDE.

Let me embrace thee most vehemently.                     160

MELANTHA (*advancing*).

I'll sacrifice my life for French poetry.

DORALICE.

I'll die upon the spot for our country wit.

---

153. boy?] *Q1–2, C1–2;* boy! *Q3–4.*
153. thee] *Q1–3, C1–2;* the *Q4.*

---

148. *bully*] good friend, fine fellow (*OED*).

150. *country*] *Works,* 11:502, argues that Melantha is adopting the
disdainful French attitude toward English heroic drama, in which case the
best reading is "country's." In the absence of any textual authority, and
from the use of the phrase "country wit" (IV.iii. 162), the distinction
would seem to be between the more fashionable city and the rude country.
Doralice earlier (IV.iii.133–134) identifies Melantha, then in disguise, as
the son of a "citizen," i.e., city dweller.

RHODOPHIL (*to* Melantha).
  Hold, hold young Mars. Palamede, draw back your hero.
PALAMEDE.
  'Tis time; I shall be drawn in for a second else at the
  wrong weapon.                                                165
MELANTHA.
  O that I were a man for thy sake!
DORALICE.
  You'll be a man as soon as I shall.

                *Enter a* Messenger *to* Rhodophil.

MESSENGER.
  Sir, the king has instant business with you.
  I saw the guard drawn up by your lieutenant
  Before the palace gate, ready to march.                      170
RHODOPHIL.
  'Tis somewhat sudden; say that I am coming.
                                          *Exit* Messenger.
  Now, Palamede, what think you of this sport?
  This is some sudden tumult: will you along?
PALAMEDE.
  Yes, yes, I will go; but the devil take me if ever I was less
  in humor. Why the pox could they not have stayed their 175
  tumult till tomorrow? Then I had done my business and
  been ready for 'em. Truth is, I had a little transitory
  crime to have committed first, and I am the worst man in
  the world at repenting till a sin be thoroughly done. But
  what shall we do with the two boys?                          180
RHODOPHIL.
  Let them take a lodging in the house till the business be
  over.
DORALICE.
  What, lie with a boy? For my part, I own it, I cannot
  endure to lie with a boy.

---

181. them] *Q1, C1–2;* 'em *Q2–4.*

---

174. *I will go.*] It should be remembered that Palamede is trying to
earn favor at court and hence is willing on these grounds to forego his
sexual adventure.

PALAMEDE.

The more's my sorrow, I cannot accommodate you with   185
a better bedfellow.

MELANTHA.

Let me die if I enter into a pair of sheets with him that
hates the French.

DORALICE.

Pish, take no care for us, but leave us in the streets; I
warrant you, as late as it is I'll find my lodging as well as   190
any drunken bully of 'em all.

RHODOPHIL *(aside).*

I'll fight in mere revenge, and wreak my passion
On all that spoil this hopeful assignation.

PALAMEDE.

I'm sure we fight in a good quarrel.

      Rogues may pretend religion and the laws,     195
      But a kind mistress is the Good Old Cause.    *Exeunt.*

[IV.iv] *Enter* Palmyra, Eubulus, Hermogenes.

PALMYRA.

You tell me wonders, that Leonidas
Is prince Theagenes, the late king's son.

EUBULUS.

It seemed as strange to him as now to you
Before I had convinced him. But besides
His great resemblance to the king his father,       5
The queen his mother lives, secured by me
In a religious house, to whom each year
I brought the news of his increasing virtues.
My last long absence from you both was caused
By wounds which in my journey I received      10
When set upon by thieves; I lost those jewels
And letters which your dying mother left.

0.1. Eubulus,] *Q1–4, C1;* Eubulus,
*and C2.*

---

196. *Good Old Cause*] the Puritan cause in the Revolution, used here
for sexual innuendo.

HERMOGENES.

    The same he means which, since brought to the king,
    Made him first know he had a child alive:
    'Twas then my care of prince Leonidas          15
    Caused me to say he was th'usurper's son
    Till, after forced by your apparent danger,
    I made the true discovery of your birth
    And once more hid my prince's.

               *Enter* Leonidas.

LEONIDAS.

    Hermogenes and Eubulus, retire;          20
    Those of our party whom I left without
    Expect your aid and counsel.        *Exeunt ambo.*

PALMYRA.

    I should, Leonidas, congratulate
    This happy change of your exalted fate;
    But, as my joy, so you my wonder move;      25
    Your looks have more of business than of love,
    And your last words some great design did show.

LEONIDAS.

    I frame not any to be hid from you.
    You, in my love, all my designs may see;
    But what have love and you designed for me?    30
    Fortune once more has set the balance right:
    First equalled us in lowness, then in height.
    Both of us have so long like gamesters thrown,
    Till fate comes round and gives to each his own.
    As fate is equal, so may love appear:        35
    Tell me at least what I must hope, or fear.

PALMYRA.

    After so many proofs, how can you call
    My love in doubt? Fear nothing, and hope—all.
    Think what a prince with honor may receive,
    Or I may give without a parent's leave.       40

---

14. he] *Q1–3, C1–2;* that he *Q4.*      38. doubt?] *Q1, C1–2;* doubt; *Q2;*
21. I] *Q1–2, C1–2;* we *Q3–4.*        doubt! *Q3–4.*

LEONIDAS.

You give and then restrain the grace you show,
As ostentatious priests, when souls they woo,
Promise their heav'n to all, but grant to few.
But do for me what I have dared for you.
I did no argument from duty bring:                    45
Duty's a name, and love's a real thing.

PALMYRA.

Man's love may, like wild torrents, overflow;
Woman's as deep, but in its banks must go.
My love is mine, and that I can impart,
But cannot give my person with my heart.              50

LEONIDAS.

Your love is then no gift:
For when the person it does not convey,
'Tis to give gold, and not to give the key.

PALMYRA.

Then ask my father.

LEONIDAS.                    He detains my throne:
Who holds back mine, will hardly give his own.        55

PALMYRA.

What then remains?

LEONIDAS.                    That I must have recourse
To arms, and take my love and crown by force.
Hermogenes is forming the design,
And with him all the brave and loyal join.

PALMYRA.

And is it thus you court Palmyra's bed?               60
Can she the murd'rer of her parent wed?
Desist from force: so much you well may give
To love, and me, to let my father live.

LEONIDAS.

Each act of mine my love to you has shown;
But you who tax my want of it have none.             65
You bid me part with you and let him live;
But they should nothing ask who nothing give.

55. Who] *Q1–2, Q4, C1–2;* Why      62. much]*Q1–2, Q4, C1–2;* much
*Q3.*                                          as *Q3.*

PALMYRA.

    I give what virtue and what duty can

    In vowing ne'er to wed another man.

LEONIDAS.

    You will be forced to be Argaleon's wife.          70

PALMYRA.

    I'll keep my promise though I lose my life.

LEONIDAS.

    Then you lose love, for which we both contend;

    For life is but the means, but love's the end.

PALMYRA.

    Our souls shall love hereafter.

LEONIDAS.                 I much fear

    That soul which could deny the body here        75

    To taste of love, would be a niggard there.

PALMYRA.

    Then 'tis past hope: our cruel fate, I see,

    Will make a sad divorce 'twixt you and me.

    For if you force employ, by heav'n I swear

    And all blessed beings—

LEONIDAS.            Your rash oath forbear.        80

PALMYRA.

    I never—

LEONIDAS.        Hold once more. But yet, as he

    Who 'scapes a dang'rous leap looks back to see,

    So I desire, now I am past my fear,

    To know what was that oath you meant to swear.

PALMYRA.

    I meant that if you hazarded your life        85

    Or sought my father's, ne'er to be your wife.

LEONIDAS.

    See now, Palmyra, how unkind you prove!

    Could you with so much ease forswear my love?

PALMYRA.

    You force me with your ruinous design.

---

82. dang'rous] *Q1–2, C2;* dangerous *Q3–4, C1.*
89. your] *Q1–2, Q4, C1–2;* you *Q3.*

LEONIDAS.

Your father's life is more your care than mine.      90

PALMYRA.

You wrong me: 'tis not, though it ought to be;
You are my care, heav'n knows, as well as he.

LEONIDAS.

If now the execution I delay,
My honor and my subjects I betray,
All is prepared for the just enterprise,      95
And the whole city will tomorrow rise.
The leaders of the party are within,
And Eubulus has sworn that he will bring
To head their arms the person of their king.

PALMYRA.

In telling this, you make me guilty too;      100
I therefore must discover what I know:
What honor bids you do, nature bids me prevent;
But kill me first, and then pursue your black intent.

LEONIDAS.

Palmyra, no; you shall not need to die;
Yet I'll not trust so strict a piety.      105
Within there.

*Enter* Eubulus.

Eubulus, a guard prepare;
Here, I commit this pris'ner to your care.

*Kisses Palmyra's hand, then gives it to* Eubulus.

PALMYRA.

Leonidas, I never thought these bands
Could e'er be giv'n me by a lover's hands.

LEONIDAS *(kneeling).*

Palmyra, thus your judge himself arraigns;      110
He who imposed these bonds still wears your chains.

90. your care] *Q1, Q3–4, C1–2;*    106. Within there] *Q1–2, C1–2;*
you care *Q2.*                *Within there (printed as S.D.) Q3–4.*
99. their king] *Q1–3, C1–2;* the    111. bonds] *Q1–2, C1;* bands
king *Q4.*                    *Q3–4, C2.*
105. I'll] *Q1–2, C1–2;* I will *Q3–4.*

101. *discover*] reveal.
108. *bands*] bonds.

When you to love or duty false must be,      ⎫
Or to your father guilty or to me,             ⎬
These chains alone remain to set you free.    ⎭

*Noise of swords clashing.*

POLYDAMAS *(within)*.

Secure these first; then search the inner room.          115

LEONIDAS.

From whence do these tumultuous clamors come?

*Enter* Hermogenes, *hastily.*

HERMOGENES.

We are betrayed, and there remains alone
This comfort, that your person is not known.

*Enter the* King, Argaleon, Rhodophil, Palamede, *guards, some like citizens as prisoners.*

POLYDAMAS.

What mean these midnight consultations here,
Where I, like an unsummoned guest, appear?               120

LEONIDAS.

Sir—

ARGALEON.   There needs no excuse; 'tis understood;
You were all watching for your prince's good.

POLYDAMAS.

My reverend city friends, you are well met!
On what great work were your grave wisdoms set?
Which of my actions were you scanning here?             125
What French invasion have you found to fear?

LEONIDAS.

They are my friends and come, sir, with intent
To take their leaves before my banishment.

---

119. S.P. POLYDAMAS] *Q1–3, C1–2;*      128. their] *Q1, Q3–4, C1–2;* there
*om. Q4.*                               *Q2.*
119. these] *C1–2;* this *Q1–4.*

---

113. *Or*] either.
122. *watching*] as in watching by the bed of a sick person.
123. *city friends*] Most editors note that the Puritan city was active in its distrust of a French alliance (which Charles II was secretly seeking) and hence distrustful of the king himself.

POLYDAMAS *(seeing* Palmyra).
    Your exile in both sexes friends can find:
    I see the ladies, like the men, are kind.                    130
PALMYRA *(kneeling)*.
    Alas, I came but—
POLYDAMAS.              Add not to your crime
    A lie: I'll hear you speak some other time.
    How? Eubulus! nor time nor thy disguise
    Can keep thee undiscovered from my eyes.
    A guard there; seize 'em all.                                135
RHODOPHIL.
    Yield, sir; what use of valor can be shown?
PALAMEDE.
    One, and unarmed, against a multitude?
LEONIDAS.
    O for a sword!

    *He reaches at one of the guard's halberds, and is seized behind.*

                    I wonnot lose my breath
    In fruitless pray'rs, but beg a speedy death.
PALMYRA.
    O spare Leonidas and punish me.                              140
POLYDAMAS.
    Mean girl, thou want'st an advocate for thee.
    Now the mysterious knot will be untied,
    Whether the young king lives, or where he died.
        Tomorrow's dawn shall the dark riddle clear,
        Crown all my joys, and dissipate my fear.                145
                                              *Exeunt omnes.*

132. hear] *Q1, Q4, C1–2;* here          138. wonnot] *this edn.;* w'not *Q1,*
*Q2–3.*                                   *C1;* wo'nt *Q2–4;* wo'noat *C2.*
138. S.P. LEONIDAS] *C1; om. Q1–4,*       144. shall] *Q1–3, C1–2;* all *Q4.*
*C2.*

---

    133. *nor time*] neither time.
    138. S.P. *Leonidas*] The absence of an S.P. here in the Qq and Cc
confuses the previous line as well, for its S.P. is "Pal." not the usual "Pala."
for Palamede or "Palm." for Palmyra. Palamede, Palmyra, and Leonidas
could each speak the line (IV.iv. 137).

# ACT V

Palamede, Straton. Palamede *with a letter in his hand.*

PALAMEDE.

This evening, sayest thou? will they both be here?

STRATON.

Yes, sir, both my old master and your mistress's father. The old gentlemen ride hard this journey; they say it shall be the last time they will see the town; and both of 'em are so pleased with this marriage which they have   5 concluded for you that I am afraid they will live some years longer to trouble you, with the joy of it.

PALAMEDE.

But this is such an unreasonable thing, to impose upon me to be married tomorrow; 'tis hurrying a man to execution without giving him time to say his prayers.  10

STRATON.

Yet if I might advise you, sir, you should not delay it; for your younger brother comes up with 'em and is got already into their favors. He has gained much upon my old master by finding fault with innkeepers' bills and by starving us and our horses to show his frugality; and he  15 is very well with your mistress's father by giving him receipts for the spleen, gout, and scurvy and other infirmities of old age.

PALAMEDE.

I'll rout him and his country education. Pox on him, I remember him before I travelled; he had nothing in him  20 but mere jocky, used to talk loud and make matches and was all for the crack of the field. Sense and wit were as much banished from his discourse as they are when the court goes out of town to a horse race. Go now and provide your master's lodgings.  25

---

1. thou?] *Q1–4, C2;* thou, *C1.*       gentleman rid *Q3–4.*
3. gentlemen ride] *Q1–2, C1–2;*

---

  21. *jocky*] characteristics of a young horse racer.
  21. *make matches*] propose races, fights, etc.
  22. *crack of the field*] favorite, one that is "cracked up" to perform well.

STRATON.

I go, sir.                            *Exit.*

PALAMEDE.

It vexes me to the heart to leave all my designs with
Doralice unfinished, to have flown her so often to a mark
and still to be bobbed at retrieve. If I had but once enjoyed her, though I could not have satisfied my stomach   30
with the feast, at least I should have relished my mouth a
little; but now—

*Enter* Philotis.

PHILOTIS.

Oh, sir, you are happily met; I was coming to find you.

PALAMEDE.

From your lady, I hope.

PHILOTIS.

Partly from her, but more especially from myself: she   35
has just now received a letter from her father with an
absolute command to dispose herself to marry you tomorrow.

PALAMEDE.

And she takes it to the death?

PHILOTIS.

Quite contrary. The letter could never have come in a   40
more lucky minute, for it found her in an ill humor with a
rival of yours, that shall be nameless, about the pronunciation of a French word.

PALAMEDE.

Count Rhodophil; never disguise it, I know the *amour.*
But I hope you took the occasion to strike in for me?    45

PHILOTIS.

It was my good fortune to do you some small service in it.
For your sake I discommended him all over: clothes,
person, humor, behavior, everything; and to sum up all,

---

36. father] *Q2–4, C1–2;* fathet *Q1.*

---

28–29. *to have flown . . . retrieve*] to have flown (like a falcon) to a
point where prey was last sighted, then to be cheated (bobbed) at the
second appearance of the prey. "Mark" is the quarry of a hawk (*OED* cites
this line.)

told her it was impossible to find a married man that was
otherwise, for they were all so mortified at home with    50
their wives' ill humors that they could never recover
themselves to be company abroad.

PALAMEDE.

Most divinely urged!

PHILOTIS.

Then I took occasion to commend your good qualities:
as the sweetness of your humor, the comeliness of your    55
person, your good mien, your valor, but above all your
liberality.

PALAMEDE.

I vow to Gad I had like to have forgot that good quality
in myself if thou hadst not remembered me on't: here
are five pieces for thee.    60

PHILOTIS.

Lord, you have the softest hand, sir! It would do a
woman good to touch it. Count Rhodophil's is not half so
soft, for I remember I felt it once when he gave me ten
pieces for my New Year's gift.

PALAMEDE.

O, I understand you, madam; you shall find my hand as    65
soft again as Count Rhodophil's. There are twenty pieces
for you: the former was but a retaining fee. Now I hope
you'll plead for me.

PHILOTIS.

Your own merits speak enough. Be sure only to ply her
with French words, and I'll warrant you'll do your busi-    70
ness. Here are a list of her phrases for this day: use 'em
to her upon all occasions, and foil her at her own
weapon, for she's like one of the old Amazons: she'll
never marry except it be the man who has first con-
quered her.    75

PALAMEDE.

I'll be sure to follow your advice: but you'll forget to
further my design.

PHILOTIS.

What, do you think I'll be ungrateful? —But, however, if

74. be the] Q1–3, C1–2; be a Q4.

you distrust my memory, put some token on my finger to
remember it by. That diamond there would do admir-   80
ably.

**PALAMEDE.**

There 'tis; and I ask your pardon heartily for calling
your memory into question. I assure you I'll trust it another time without putting you to the trouble of another
token.                                                       85

Enter Palmyra and Artemis.

**ARTEMIS.**

Madam, this way the prisoners are to pass;
Here you may see Leonidas.

**PALMYRA.**

Then here I'll stay and follow him to death.

Enter Melantha hastily.

**MELANTHA.**

O, here's her highness! Now is my time to introduce
myself and to make my court to her in my new French  90
phrases. Stay, let me read my catalogue—*suite, figure,
chagrin, naiveté,* and *let me die* for the parenthesis of all.

**PALAMEDE** *(aside).*

Do, persecute her, and I'll persecute thee as fast in thy
own dialect.

**MELANTHA.**

Madam, the princess! let me die but this is a most horrid  95
spectacle, to see a person who makes so grand a *figure* in
the court without the *suite* of a princess, and entertaining
your *chagrin* all alone. —[*Aside.*] *Naiveté* should have
been there, but the disobedient word would not come in.

**PALMYRA.**

What is she, Artemis?                                       100

89. highness! Now] *this edn.;*
highness!/ Now *(printed as verse)*
*Q1–4, C1–2.*
92. *naiveté,* and *let me die*] *Q4,*
*C1–2; naivete,* and let me die *Q1–3.*

95. Madam,] *Q1 (but poorly inked in
some copies), C2;* Madam *Q2–4, C1.*
96, 107, 125. *figure*] *this edn.;* figure *Q1–4, C1–2.*

ARTEMIS.
An impertinent lady, madam, very ambitious of being
known to your highness.

PALAMEDE (*to* Melantha).

Let me die, madam, if I have not waited you here these
two long hours without so much as the *suite* of a single
servant to attend me, entertaining myself with my own 105
*chagrin* till I had the honor to see your ladyship, who are
a person that makes so considerable a *figure* in the court.

MELANTHA.
Truce with your *doceurs*, good servant; you see I am addressing to the princess; pray do not *embarrass* me—*Embarrass* me! what a delicious French word do you make 110
me lose upon you too! *(To the* Princess.) Your highness,
madam, will please to pardon the *bévue* which I made in
not sooner finding you out to be a princess. But let me
die if this *éclaircissement* which is made this day of your
quality does not ravish me; and give me leave to tell 115
you—

PALAMEDE.
But first give me leave to tell you, madam, that I have so
great a *tendre* for your person and such a *penchant* to do
you service, that—

MELANTHA.
What, must I still be troubled with your *sottises*? (There's 120
another word lost that I meant for the princess, with a
mischief to you.) —But your highness, madam—

PALAMEDE.
But your ladyship, madam—

*Enter* Leonidas *guarded, and led over the stage.*

109. to the] *Q1–3, C1–2;* the *Q4.*          *Q1–2, C1–2; pauchant Q3–4.*
118. *tendre*] *this edn.;* tender *Q1–4,*      123.1. *led*] *Q1, Q4, C1–2;* lead
*C1–2.*                                         *Q2–3.*
118. *penchant*] *this edn.;* panchant

112. *bévue*] blunder, slip.
114. *this day*] actually, the previous day. See V.323.
120. *sottises*] foolishness, nonsense.

MELANTHA.

Out upon him, how he looks, madam! now he's found no
prince, he is the strangest *figure* of a man; how could I   125
make that *coup d'étourdi* to think him one?

PALMYRA.

Away, impertinent. —My dear Leonidas!

LEONIDAS.

My dear Palmyra!

PALMYRA.

Death shall never part us; my destiny is yours.

*He is led off; she follows.*

MELANTHA.

Impertinent! O, I am the most unfortunate person this   130
day breathing. That the princess should thus *rompre en
visière,* without occasion. Let me die but I'll follow her to
death till I make my peace.

PALAMEDE *(holding her).*

And let me die, but I'll follow you to the infernals till you
pity me.                                                  135

MELANTHA *(turning toward him angrily).*

Ay, 'tis long of you that this *malheur* is fallen upon me;
your impertinence has put me out of the good *grâces* of
the princess, and all that, which has ruined me, and all
that, and therefore let me die but I'll be revenged, and
all that.                                                 140

PALAMEDE.

*Façon, façon;* you must and shall love me, and all that; for
my old man is coming up, and all that; and I am *désespéré
au dernier,* and will not be disinherited, and all that.

---

129. us; my] *C2;* us;/ My *(printed as*          *rampre Q2.*
*two lines) Q1–4, C1.*                             137. *grâces*] *this edn.;* graces *Q1–4,*
131. *rompre*]   *Q1,*   *Q3–4,*   *C1–2;*         *C1–2.*

---

126. *coup d'étourdi*] heedlessness, thoughtlessness, giddy act.
131–132. *rompre en visière*] break with [me]; take offense; literally,
break from the mask [of social etiquette].
136. *long of*] because of *(OED).*
136. *malheur*] misfortune.
141. *Façon, façon*] stuff and nonsense.
142–143. *désespéré au denier*] desperate to the utmost.

MELANTHA.
How durst you interrupt me so *mal à propos* when you
knew I was addressing to the princess?    145
PALAMEDE.
But why would you address yourself so much *à contre-
temps* then?
MELANTHA.
Ah, *male peste!*
PALAMEDE.
Ah, *j'enrage!*
PHILOTIS.
*Radoucissez vous, de grâce, madame; vous êtes bien en colère* 150
*pour peu de chose. Vous n'entendez pas la raillerie galante.*
MELANTHA.
*À d'autres, à d'autres.* He mocks himself of me, he abuses
me: ah me unfortunate!    *Cries.*
PHILOTIS.
You mistake him, madam; he does but accommodate his
phrase to your refined language. *Ah, qu'il est un cavalier* 155
*accompli!– (To him.)* Pursue your point, sir.
PALAMEDE *(singing).*
*Ah, qu'il fait beau dans ces bocages;*

---

149. *j'enrage*] this edn.; *I'enrage Q1,*    153. S.D. *Cries.*] *C2; cries! Q1–4,*
*C1; l'enrage Q2; l'enrage Q3–4;*    *C1.*
*J'enrage C2.*

---

146–147. *à contretemps*] at the wrong time.
150–151. *Radoucissez . . . galante*] Pray, madam, calm yourself; you're
in a state over nothing. You misunderstand gallant raillery.
152. *À d'autres, à d'autres*] "go on," tell it to someone else.
152. *He mocks himself of me*] Sutherland, p. 149, notes that the syntax
is French.
157–158. *Ah, qu'il . . . jour*] These lines and those that follow (164–
166) occur in a song from Molière's *Le bourgeois gentilhomme* (1670). An
eighteenth-century bilingual edition (1732) cited in *Works*, 11:503–504,
translates the first four lines as the following eight: "What pleasures in these
thickets dwell!/ How genial Phoebus cheers the day!/ (*Another man.*). Whilst,
in the spray, sweet Philomel/ Alternate to the echo tunes her lay./ This sweet
abode,/ This pleasant grove,/ This sweet abode,/ Invites to love." Lines
three and four suggest Melantha's echoing, ll. 165–166.

*Ah que le ciel donne un beau jour!*
There I was with you, with a *minuet*.

MELANTHA *(laughs).*
Let me die now, but this singing is fine and extremely 160
French in him.—*(Crying).*  But then, that he should use
my own words, as it were in contempt of me, I cannot
bear it.

PALAMEDE *(singing).*
*Ces beaux séjours, ces doux ramages—*

MELANTHA *(singing after him).*
*Ces beaux séjours, ces doux ramages,*                    165
*Ces beaux séjours nous invitent à l'amour.*
*(Laughing.)*   Let me die but he sings *en cavalier* and so
humors the cadence.

PALAMEDE *(singing).*
*Vois, ma Climène, vois sous ce chêne.*
*S'entrebaiser ces oiseaux amoureux!*                     170
Let me die now, but that was fine. Ah now, for three or
four brisk Frenchmen to be put into masking habits and
to sing it on a theater, how witty it would be! and then to
dance helter skelter to a *chanson à boire:*
*Toute la terre, toute la terre est a moi!*               175
What's matter though it were made and sung two or
three years ago in *cabarets:* how it would attract the admiration, especially of everyone that's an *éveillé!*

MELANTHA.
Well, I begin to have a *tendre* for you; but yet, upon
condition that—when we are married, you—             180

179. *tendre*] *this edn.;* tender *Q1–4,*
*C1–2.*

---

160. *fine*] Perhaps Melantha says "*fin*" (refined), as might Palamede, l.
171.
167. *en cavalier*] in a gallant manner.
168. *humors*] accommodates himself to *(OED).*
169–170. *Vois . . . amoureaux*] another song from *Le bourgeois gen-*
*tilhomme,* translated in 1732 as "See, my Clemene, see/ Under yon spread-
ing tree,/ The amorous turtles coo and bill . . . " *(Works,* 11:504).
174. *chanson à boire*] drinking song.
175. *Toute . . . moi*] source unidentified ("All the world is mine").
178. *éveillé*] lively, up-to-date (the noun is *éveilleur*).
180, 185. *condition*] Perhaps Melantha uses a French pronunciation,
as might Philotis (l. 182) and Palamede (l. 186).

PHILOTIS [*to him*].

You must drown her voice: if she makes her French
conditions you are a slave forever.

Palamede *sings while she speaks.*

MELANTHA.

First, will you engage that—

PALAMEDE (*louder*).

Fa, la, la, la, etc.

MELANTHA.

Will you hear the conditions?                               185

PALAMEDE.

No, I will hear no conditions! I am resolved to win you *en
français*, to be very airy, with abundance of noise, and no
sense. Fa, la, la, la, etc.

MELANTHA.

Hold, hold: I am vanquished with your *gaîté d'esprit*. I am
yours, and will be yours, *sans nulle réserve, ni condition*. 190
And let me die, if I do not think myself the happiest
nymph in Sicily.—My dear French dear, stay but a *minute*
till I *raccommode* myself with the princess, and then I am
yours *jusqu'à la mort. Allons donc*–

Exeunt Melantha, Philotis.

PALAMEDE (*solus, fanning himself with his hat*).

I never thought before that wooing was so laborious an 195
exercise; if she were worth a million, I have deserved
her; and now, methinks too, with taking all this pains for
her I begin to like her. 'Tis so. I have known many who
never cared for hare nor partridge, but those they
caught themselves would eat heartily: the pains, and the 200
story a man tells of taking of 'em, makes the meat go
down more pleasantly. Besides, last night I had a sweet
dream of her and, Gad, she I have once dreamed of, I
am stark mad till I enjoy her, let her be never so ugly.

---

192–193. *minute*] spelled *miniute* in Qq, Cc: "This error for *minute*
may suggest Melantha's imperfect command of French" (B-B, p. 351).

193. *raccommode*] mend, reconcile.

194. *jusqu'à la mort*] until death.

*Enter* Doralice.

DORALICE.

Who's that you are so mad to enjoy, Palamede?       205

PALAMEDE.

You may easily imagine that, sweet Doralice.

DORALICE.

More easily than you think I can. I met just now with a
certain man who came to you with letters, from a certain
old gentleman, yclept your father, whereby I am given to
understand that tomorrow you are to take an oath in the 210
church to be grave henceforward, to go ill-dressed and
slovenly, to get heirs for your estate, and to dandle 'em
for your diversion; and, in short, that love and courtship
are to be no more.

PALAMEDE.

Now have I so much shame to be thus apprehended in 215
the manner that I can neither speak nor look upon you. I
have abundance of grace in me, that I find. But if you
have any spark of true friendship in you, retire a little
with me to the next room that has a couch or bed in't,
and bestow your charity upon a poor dying man: a little 220
comfort from a mistress before a man is going to give
himself in marriage is as good as a lusty dose of strong
water to a dying malefactor: it takes away the sense of
hell and hanging from him.

DORALICE.

No, good Palamede, I must not be so injurious to your 225
bride: 'tis ill drawing from the bank today when all your
ready money is payable tomorrow.

PALAMEDE.

A wife is only to have the ripe fruit that falls of itself; but
a wise man will always preserve a shaking for a mistress.

DORALICE.

But a wife for the first quarter is a mistress.       230

208. from] *Q1, Q3–4, C1–2;* form    222. in] *Q1–3, C1–2;* into *Q4.*
*Q2.*

---

222–223. *strong  water . . . malefactor*] Condemned criminals were
offered alcoholic spirits on their way to the gallows (Summers, 3:549–
550).
    230. *quarter . . . mistress*] The "natural term of any mistress" is a
quarter year (I.156).

PALAMEDE.

But when the second comes—

DORALICE.

When it does come, you are so given to variety that you would make a wife of me in another quarter.

PALAMEDE.

No, never, except I were married to you. Married people can never oblige one another, for all they do is duty, and 235 consequently there can be no thanks. But love is more frank and generous than he is honest: he's a liberal giver, but a cursed paymaster.

DORALICE.

I declare I will have no gallant; but if I would, he should never be a married man; a married man is but a mis- 240 tress's half-servant, as a clergyman is but the king's half-subject. For a man to come to me that smells o' th' wife! 'S life, I would as soon wear her old gown after her as her husband.

PALAMEDE.

Yet 'tis a kind of fashion to wear a princess's cast shoes; 245 you see the country ladies buy 'em to be fine in them.

DORALICE.

Yes, a princess's shoes may be worn after her, because they keep their fashion by being so very little used; but generally a married man is the creature of the world the most out of fashion; his behavior is dumpish, his dis- 250 course his wife and family, his habit so much neglected it looks as if that were married too: his hat is married, his peruke is married, his breeches are married, and if we could look within his breeches, we should find him married there too.                                                   255

PALAMEDE.

Am I then to be discarded forever? Pray do but mark how terrible that word sounds. Forever! it has a very damned sound, Doralice.

DORALICE.

Ay, forever! It sounds as hellishly to me as it can do to you, but there's no help for't.                                    260

---

243, 245. wear] *Q1, Q3–4, C1–2;*      249. is the] *Q1–2, C1–2;* is a *Q3–4.*
were *Q2.*                             252. if that] *Q1–3, C1–2;* if it *Q4.*
246. them] *Q1–4, C2;* 'em *C1.*

PALAMEDE.

Yet if we had but once enjoyed one another—but then once only is worse than not at all: it leaves a man with such a lingering after it.

DORALICE.

For aught I know 'tis better that we have not; we might upon trial have liked each other less, as many a man and 265 woman that have loved as desperately as we, and yet when they came to possession, have sighed and cried to themselves "Is this all?"

PALAMEDE.

That is only if the servant were not found a man of this world. But if upon trial we had not liked each other, we 270 had certainly left loving; and faith, that's the greater happiness of the two.

DORALICE.

'Tis better as 'tis; we have drawn off already as much of our love as would run clear; after possessing, the rest is but jealousies and disquiets and quarreling and piecing. 275

PALAMEDE.

Nay, after one great quarrel there's never any sound piecing; the love is apt to break in the same place again.

DORALICE.

I declare I would never renew a love; that's like him who trims an old coach ten years together: he might buy a new one better cheap.                                    280

PALAMEDE.

Well, madam, I am convinced that 'tis best for us not to have enjoyed; but Gad, the strongest reason is because I can't help it.

DORALICE.

The only way to keep us new to one another is never to

276.  one] *Q1, Q3–4, C1–2;* on *Q2.*
279.  years] *Q1, Q3–4, C1–2;* yers
*Q2.*

---

273–274. *drawn off . . . run clear*] Doralice's metaphor concerns the decanting from kegs of liquids containing sediments, such as cider, beer, or wine.

275. *piecing*] "making up, with plays upon 'mending' and 'making peace' " (*Works*, 11:504).

enjoy, as they keep grapes by hanging 'em upon a line: 285
they must touch nothing if you would preserve 'em
fresh.

PALAMEDE.

But then they wither and grow dry in the very keeping;
however, I shall have a warmth for you, and an eagerness, every time I see you; and if I chance to outlive 290
Melantha—

DORALICE.

And if I chance to outlive Rhodophil—

PALAMEDE.

Well, I'll cherish my body as much as I can upon that
hope. 'Tis true I would not directly murder the wife of
my bosom; but to kill her civilly, by the way of kindness, 295
I'll put as fair as another man: I'll begin tomorrow night
and be very wrathful with her, that's resolved on.

DORALICE.

Well, Palamede, here's my hand: I'll venture to be your
second wife, for all your threatenings.

PALAMEDE.

In the meantime I'll watch you hourly as I would the 300
ripeness of a melon; and I hope you'll give me leave now
and then to look on you, and to see if you are not ready
to be cut yet.

DORALICE.

No, no, that must not be, Palamede, for fear the gar-
dener should come and catch you taking up the glass.  305

*Enter* Rhodophil.

---

285. grapes] *Q1–4, C1;* grapes; *C2.*      305. come and catch you taking]
296. fair] *Q1, C1–2;* fare *Q2;* far      *Q1, C2;* come and catch you a
*Q3–4.*                                     taking *Q2–4;* catch you taking *C1.*

   295. *to kill . . . kindness*] proverbial from at least 1558 (Tilley). Cf.
Thomas Heywood's play, *A Woman Killed with Kindness* (1607).
   296. *put*] Palamede uses a sexual pun: "to thrust or plunge (a
weapon) home or into a body" (*OED* B.I.3).
   301–305. *melon . . . glass*] Sutherland, p. 149, notes that *melon* might
mean vegetables as different as pumpkins and muskmelons; Doralice's
rejoinder suggests a delicate crop with a long growing season such as
might be nurtured in a cold frame or hot house.

RHODOPHIL (*aside*).

Billing so sweetly! now I am confirmed in my suspicions;
I must put an end to this ere it go further. (*To* Doralice.)   Cry you mercy, spouse; I fear I have interrupted
your recreations.

DORALICE.

What recreations?                                              310

RHODOPHIL.

Nay, no excuses, good spouse; I saw fair hand conveyed
to lip, and pressed, as though you had been squeezing
soft wax together for an indenture. Palamede, you and I
must clear this reckoning: why would you have seduced
my wife?                                                       315

PALAMEDE.

Why would you have debauched my mistress?

RHODOPHIL.

What do you think of that civil couple that played at a
game called "Hide and Seek" last evening in the grotto?

PALAMEDE.

What do you think of that innocent pair who made it
their pretense to seek for others, but came, indeed, to 320
hide themselves there?

RHODOPHIL.

All things considered, I begin vehemently to suspect that
the young gentleman I found in your company last night
was a certain youth of my acquaintance.

PALAMEDE.

And I have an odd imagination that you could never 325
have suspected my small gallant if your little villainous
Frenchman had not been a false brother.

RHODOPHIL.

Farther arguments are needless. Draw off; I shall speak
to you now by the way of *bilbo*.   *Claps his hand to his sword.*

---

307. an end] *Q1–3, C2;* and end     308. Cry you] *Q1–3, C1–2;* Cry
*Q4;* en end *C1.*                    your *Q4.*

---

313. *indenture*] "impression, with a play on sealing an agreement"
(B-B, p. 354).
329. *bilbo*] a sword; the blades manufactured in Bilbao, Spain, were
noted for their temper and elasticity.

PALAMEDE.

And I shall answer you by the way of Dangerfield.     330

*Claps his hand on his.*

DORALICE.

Hold, hold; are not you two a couple of mad fighting
fools, to cut one another's throats for nothing?

PALAMEDE.

How for nothing? He courts the woman I must marry.

RHODOPHIL.

And he courts you whom I have married.

DORALICE.

But you can neither of you be jealous of what you love     335
not.

RHODOPHIL.

Faith I am jealous, and that makes me partly suspect that
I love you better than I thought.

DORALICE.

Pish! a mere jealousy of honor.

RHODOPHIL.

Gad I am afraid there's something else in't; for Palamede     340
has wit, and if he loves you, there's something more in ye
than I have found, some rich mine, for aught I know,
that I have not yet discovered.

PALAMEDE.

'S life, what's this? here's an argument for me to love
Melantha; for he has loved her, and he has wit too, and     345
for aught I know, there may be a mine: but if there be, I
am resolved to dig for it.

DORALICE (*to* Rhodophil).

Then I have found my account in raising your jealousy:
O! 'tis the most delicate sharp sauce to a cloyed stomach;
it will give you a new edge, Rhodophil.     350

RHODOPHIL.

And a new point too, Doralice, if I could be sure thou art
honest.

339. S.P. DORALICE] *Q1–2, C1–2;*     *Q4.*
PALAMEDE *Q3–4.*                                          341. in ye] *Q1–3, C1–2;* in you *Q4.*
340. there's] *Q1–3, C1–2;* there is

330. *Dangerfield*] conventional name for a sword-carrying bully and
braggart.

DORALICE.

If you are wise, believe me for your own sake. Love and religion have but one thing to trust to; that's a good sound faith. Consider, if I have played false, you can 355 never find it out by any experiment you can make upon me.

RHODOPHIL.

No? Why, suppose I had a delicate screwed gun: if I left her clean and found her foul, I should discover to my cost she had been shot in.                    360

DORALICE.

But if you left her clean and found her only rusty, you would discover to your shame she was only so for want of shooting.

PALAMEDE.

Rhodophil, you know me too well to imagine I speak for fear; and therefore in consideration of our past friend- 365 ship, I will tell you, and bind it by all things holy, that Doralice is innocent.

RHODOPHIL.

Friend, I will believe you, and vow the same for your Melantha; but the devil on't is, how shall we keep 'em so?

PALAMEDE.

What dost think of a blessed community betwixt us four, 370 for the solace of the women and relief of the men? Methinks it would be a pleasant kind of life: wife and husband for the standing dish, and mistress and gallant for the dessert.

RHODOPHIL.

But suppose the wife and the mistress should both long 375 for the standing dish: how should they be satisfied together?

PALAMEDE.

In such a case they must draw lots. And yet that would

353. are] *Q1–2, Q4, C1–2;* art *Q3.*
369. so?] *Q2–4;* so. *Q1, C1–2.*

---

358. *delicate screwed gun*] a gun with a finely grooved bore; a rifle.
373, 376. *standing dish*] a dish that appears regularly every day or every meal.

not do neither, for they would both be wishing for the
longest cut.                                                    380

RHODOPHIL.

Then I think, Palamede, we had as good make a firm
league not to invade each other's propriety.

PALAMEDE.

Content, say I. From henceforth let all acts of hostility
cease betwixt us, and that in the usual form of treaties, as
well by sea as by land, and in all fresh waters.               385

DORALICE.

I will add but one proviso: that whoever breaks the
league, either by war abroad or by neglect at home, both
the women shall revenge themselves by the help of the
other party.

RHODOPHIL.

That's but reasonable. Come away, Doralice; I have a     390
great temptation to be sealing articles in private.

PALAMEDE (*claps him on the shoulder*).

Hast thou so?
    Fall on, Macduff,
And curst be he that first cries, "Hold, enough."

*Enter* Polydamas, Palmyra, Artemis, Argaleon: *after them,* Eubulus
*and* Hermogenes, *guarded.*

PALMYRA.

Sir, on my knees I beg you.                                     395

POLYDAMAS.

Away, I'll hear no more.

PALMYRA.

For my dead mother's sake; you say you loved her,

---

379. both be] *Q1–2, C1–2;* be both          386. but one] *Q1–3, C1–2;* one *Q4.*
*Q3–4.*                                       396. hear] *Q1, Q3–4, C1–2;* here
380. cut.] *C1, Sutherland, Works;*           *Q2.*
out? *Q1;* out. *Q2–4, C2;* cut! *B-B.*
385. as by] *Q1–4, C2;* as *C1.*

---

382. *propriety*] property.
393–394. *Fall on . . . enough*] a misquotation of Macbeth's challenge
in Shakespeare's play, V.iii.33–34.

And tell me I resemble her. Thus she
Had begged.

POLYDAMAS.        And thus had I denied her.

PALMYRA.
You must be merciful.

ARGALEON.              You must be constant.        400

POLYDAMAS.
Go, bear 'em to the torture; you have boasted
You have a king to head you: I would know
To whom I must resign.

EUBULUS.                This is our recompense
For serving thy dead queen.

HERMOGENES.              And education
Of thy daughter.        405

ARGALEON.
You are too modest in not naming all
His obligations to you: why did you
Omit his son, the prince Leonidas?

POLYDAMAS.
That imposture
I had forgot; their tortures shall be doubled.        410

HERMOGENES.
You please me, I shall die the sooner.

EUBULUS.
No, could I live an age and still be racked,
I still would keep the secret.

*As they are going off, enter* Leonidas, *guarded*.

LEONIDAS.
O, whither do you hurry innocence?
If you have any justice, spare their lives;        415
Or if I cannot make you just, at least
I'll teach you to more purpose to be cruel.

PALMYRA.
Alas, what does he seek?

398–399. her. Thus she/ Had]
*Q1–4, C1–2, Sutherland, Works;* her./
Thus she had *B-B.*
404. thy] *Q1, C1–2;* the *Q2–4.*

414. innocence?] *Works;* innocence! *Q1–4, C1–2, Sutherland, B-B.*
418. seek?] *Works;* seek! *Q1–4,
C1–2, Sutherland, B-B.*

LEONIDAS.

Make me the object of your hate and vengeance!
Are these decrepit bodies worn to ruin,                    420
Just ready of themselves to fall asunder
And to let drop the soul,
Are these fit subjects for a rack and tortures?
Where would you fasten any hold upon 'em?
Place pains on me; united fix 'em here;                    425
I have both youth and strength and soul to bear 'em:
And if they merit death, then I much more,
Since 'tis for me they suffer.

HERMOGENES.                    Heav'n forbid
We should redeem our pains or worthless lives
By our exposing yours.                    430

EUBULUS.

Away with us. Farewell, sir.
I only suffer in my fears for you.

ARGALEON (aside).

So much concerned for him? then my
Suspicion's true.                    *Whispers the* King.

PALMYRA.

Hear yet my last request, for poor Leonidas,                    435
Or take my life with his.

ARGALEON (to the King).

Rest satisfied: Leonidas is he.

POLYDAMAS [to Argaleon].

I am amazed: what must be done?

ARGALEON [to him].

Command his execution instantly;
Give him not leisure to discover it;                    440
He may corrupt the soldiers.

POLYDAMAS.

Hence with that traitor; bear him to his death.
Haste there, and see my will performed.

---

419. vengeance!] *Q1, C1–2;* vengeance *Q2–4.*
424. 'em?] *Q1–3, C1–2;* 'em: *Q4.*
433–434. him? then my/ Suspicion's] *Q1–4, C1–2, Works;* him?

. . . true *(i.e., one line)* Sutherland;
him?/ Then . . . *B.B.*
435. Hear] *Q1, Q3–4, C1–2;* Here
*Q2.*

LEONIDAS.

Nay, then I'll die like him the gods have made me.

Hold, gentlemen, I am—                                           445

Argaleon *stops his mouth.*

ARGALEON.

Thou art a traitor; 'tis not fit to hear thee.

LEONIDAS (*getting loose a little*).

I say I am the—

ARGALEON (*again stopping his mouth*).

So; gag him, and lead him off.

Leonidas, Hermogenes, Eubulus *led off.* Polydamas *and* Argaleon
*follow.*

PALMYRA.

Duty and love by turns possess my soul,

And struggle for a fatal victory.                                450

I will discover he's the king. Ah, no:

That will perhaps save him,

But then I am guilty of a father's ruin.

What shall I do, or not do? Either way

I must destroy a parent or a lover.                              455

Break heart, for that's the least of ills to me,

And death the only cure.                              *Swoons.*

ARTEMIS.                          Help, help the princess.

RHODOPHIL.

Bear her gently hence,

Where she may have more succor.

*She is borne off;* Artemis *follows her. Shouts within, and clashing of
swords.*

PALAMEDE.

What noise is that?                                               460

*Enter* Amalthea, *running.*

AMALTHEA.

O, gentlemen, if you have loyalty

---

458–459. Bear . . . hence, /Where        more *Q1–4, C1–2;* Bear . . . may
she may have more succor] *Suther-*       have/ More *Works.*
*land,* B-B;     Bear . . . may/Have

451. *discover*] reveal.

Or courage, show it now: Leonidas
Broke on the sudden from his guards, and snatching
A sword from one, his back against the scaffold,
Bravely defends himself, and owns aloud                      465
He is our long-lost king, found for this moment,
But if your valors help not, lost forever.
Two of his guards, moved by the sense of virtue,
Are turned for him, and there they stand at bay
Against an host of foes.
RHODOPHIL.                          Madam, no more;          470
We lose time: my command, or my example,
May move the soldiers to the better cause.
(*To* Palamede).   You'll second me?
PALAMEDE.
Or die with you: no subject e'er can meet
A nobler fate, than at his sovereign's feet.        *Exeunt.* 475

*Clashing of swords within, and shouts. Enter* Leonidas, Rhodophil,
Palamede, Eubulus, Hermogenes, *and their party, victorious;*
Polydamas *and* Argaleon, *disarmed.*

LEONIDAS.
That I survive the dangers of this day,
Next to the gods, brave friends, be yours the honor.
And let heav'n witness for me, that my joy
Is not more great for this my right restored,
Than 'tis that I have power to recompense                    480
Your loyalty and valor. Let mean princes
Of abject souls fear to reward great actions;
I mean to show
That whatsoe'er subjects like you dare merit,
A king like me dares give.                                   485
RHODOPHIL.
You make us blush; we have deserved so little.
PALAMEDE.
And yet instruct us how to merit more.
LEONIDAS.
And as I would be just in my rewards,

478.  heav'n] *Q1–4, C2;* heaven *C1.*

So should I in my punishments; these two,
This the usurper of my crown, the other                    490
Of my Palmyra's love, deserve that death
Which both designed for me.
POLYDAMAS.                              And we expect it.
ARGALEON.
I have too long been happy to live wretched.
POLYDAMAS.
And I too long have governed to desire
A life without an empire.                                  495
LEONIDAS.
You are Palmyra's father, and as such,
Though not a king, shall have obedience paid
From him who is one. Father, in that name,
All injury's forgot, and duty owned.          *Embraces him.*
POLYDAMAS.
O, had I known you could have been this king,              500
Thus godlike, great, and good, I should have wished
T'have been dethroned before. 'Tis now I live
And more than reign; now all my joys flow pure,
Unmixed with cares, and undisturbed by conscience.

*Enter* Palmyra, Amalthea, Artemis, Doralice, *and* Melantha.

LEONIDAS.
See, my Palmyra comes! the frighted blood                  505
Scarce yet recalled to her pale cheeks,
Like the first streaks of light broke loose from darkness
And dawning into blushes. —(*To* Polydamas.)   Sir, you
    said
Your joys were full; O, would you make mine so!
I am but half restored without this blessing.             510
POLYDAMAS.
The gods, and my Palmyra, make you happy,

490. This the] *Q1–3, C1–2;* This is      509. were] *Q1–3, C1–2;* are *Q4.*
the *Q4.*                                  511. and] *Q1–3, C1–2;* and, and
502. before.] *Q1–4. C2;* before!   *Q4.*
*C1.*

---

499. *injury's*] Sutherland, p. 150, suggests but does not print the
emendation "injury's" for the Qq, Cc reading "injuries."

As you make me.                 *Gives her hand to* Leonidas.
PALMYRA.          Now all my pray'rs are heard:
I may be dutiful and yet may love.
Virtue and patience have at length unravelled
The knots which fortune tied.                    515
MELANTHA.
Let me die, but I'll congratulate his majesty. How
admirably well his royalty becomes him! Becomes! that is
*lui sied,* but our damned language expresses nothing.
PALAMEDE.
How? does it become him already? 'twas but just now you
said he was such a *figure* of a man.                    520
MELANTHA.
True, my dear, when he was a private man he was a
*figure*; but since he is a king, methinks he has assumed
another *figure*: he looks so grand and so august.
                              *Going to the* King.
PALAMEDE.
Stay, stay, I'll present you when it is more convenient.
—[*Aside.*]   I find I must get her a place at court; and 525
when she is once there, she can be no longer ridiculous;
for she is young enough, and pretty enough, and fool
enough, and French enough, to bring up a fashion there
to be affected.
LEONIDAS (*to* Rhodophil).
Did she then lead you to this brave attempt?                    530
(*To* Amalthea.)   To you, fair Amalthea, what I am,
And what all these from me, we jointly owe.
First, therefore, to your great desert we give
Your brother's life; but keep him under guard
Till our new power be settled. What more grace                    535

512. pray'rs] *C1;* prayers *Q1–4,*      520. was such] *Q1–3, C1–2;* was
*C2.*                                     *Q4.*
516–518. Let me die . . .nothing]        520, 522, 523. *figure*] *this edn.;*
*this edn.; printed as verse Q1–4, C1–2*  figure *Q1–4, C1–2.*
(his/    Majesty . . . royalty/    Be-   533. we give] *Q1, C1–2;* give *Q2–3;*
comes . . .).                            I give *Q4.*

518. *lui sied*] it becomes him (from *seoir,* to suit, to become).
533. *desert*] deserving.

He may receive shall from his future carriage
Be given, as he deserves.

ARGALEON.

I neither now desire nor will deserve it;
My loss is such as cannot be repaired,
And to the wretched, life can be no mercy.                    540

LEONIDAS.

Then be a prisoner always: thy ill fate
And pride will have it so. But since in this I cannot,
Instruct me, generous Amalthea, how
A king may serve you.

AMALTHEA.                I have all I hope
And all I now must wish: I see you happy.                    545
Those hours I have to live, which heav'n in pity
Will make but few, I vow to spend with vestals,
The greatest part in pray'rs for you, the rest
In mourning my unworthiness.
Press me not farther to explain myself:                      550
'Twill not become me, and may cause you trouble.

LEONIDAS (aside).

Too well I understand her secret grief,
But dare not seem to know it. —(To Palmyra.)   Come
     my fairest,
Beyond my crown I have one joy in store:
To give that crown to her whom I adore.                      555

*Exeunt omnes.*

544. all I hope] *Q1–3, C1–2;* all
hope *Q4.*
550. not] *Q1–3, C1–2;* no *Q4.*
551. you trouble] *Sutherland, B-B,
Works;* your trouble *Q1–4, C1–2.*

# EPILOGUE

Thus have my spouse and I informed the nation
And led you all the way to reformation,
Not with dull morals, gravely writ, like those
Which men of easy phlegm with care compose—
Your poets of still words and limber sense,                     5
Born on the confines of indifference—
But by examples drawn, I dare to say,
From most of you who hear and see the play.
There are more Rhodophils in this theater,
More Palamedes, and some few wives, I fear.                     10
But yet too far our poet would not run;
Though 'twas well offered, there was nothing done.
He could not quite the women's frailty bare,
But stript 'em to the waist, and left 'em there;
And the men's faults are less severely shown,                   15
For he considers that himself is one.
Some stabbing wits, to bloody satire bent,
Would treat both sexes with less compliment,
Would lay the scene at home, of husbands tell,
For wenches taking up their wives i' th' Mell,                  20
And a brisk bout which each of them did want,
Made by mistake of mistress and gallant.
Our modest author thought it was enough
To cut you off a sample of the stuff:
He spared my shame, which you, I'm sure, would not,            25
For you were all for driving on the plot.
You sighed when I came in to break the sport,
And set your teeth when each design fell short.
To wives and servants all good wishes lend,

---

5. poets] *Sutherland, Works;* poet's    13. women's] *Sutherland,*    B-B,
*Q1–4, C1–2, B-B.*                       *Works;* woman's *Q1–4, C1–2.*

---

0.1. EPILOGUE] spoken in character by Rhodophil.
4. *men of easy phlegm*] phlegmatic or dull, sluggish men.
5. *limber*] limp, flaccid, flabby (*OED* 1.c).
20. *Mell*] the Mall, a fashionable walk along St. James Park.

But the poor cuckold seldom finds a friend.          30
Since therefore court and town will take no pity,
I humbly cast myself upon the city.

---

32. *city*] the mercantile center of London whose wives were fair
game to the court wits.

# Appendix

## Chronology

Approximate dates are indicated by *. Dates for plays are those on which they were first made public, either on stage or in print.

| Political and Literary Events | Life and Major Works of Dryden |
|---|---|
| 1631 | |
| Death of Donne. | Born in Aldwinckle, Northamptonshire, August 9. |
| 1633 | |
| Samuel Pepys born. | |
| 1635 | |
| Sir George Etherege born.* | |
| 1640 | |
| Aphra Behn born.* | |
| 1641 | |
| William Wycherley born.* | |
| 1642 | |
| First Civil War began (ended 1646). | |
| Theaters closed by Parliament. | |
| Thomas Shadwell born.* | |
| 1646 | |
| | Became a King's Scholar at Westminster School, London.* |
| 1648 | |
| Second Civil War. | |
| Nathaniel Lee born.* | |
| 1649 | |
| Execution of Charles I. | *Upon the Death of the Lord Hastings* published. |
| 1650 | |
| Jeremy Collier born. | Admitted to Trinity College, Cambridge, on May 18. |
| | *To John Hoddeston, on His Divine Epigrams* published. |

1651
Hobbes's *Leviathan* published.

1652
First Dutch War began (ended
1654).
Thomas Otway born.

1654

B.A., left Cambridge in March.
His father died in June.

1656
D'Avenant's *THE SIEGE OF
RHODES* performed at Rutland
House.

Employed by Cromwell's government (until 1658).

1657
John Dennis born.

1658
Death of Oliver Cromwell.
D'Avenant's *THE CRUELTY OF
THE SPANIARDS IN PERU* per-
formed at the Cockpit.

1659

*Heroic Stanzas to the Glorious
Memory of Cromwell* published.

1660
Restoration of Charles II.
Theatrical patents granted to
Thomas Killigrew and Sir William D'Avenant, authorizing them
to form, respectively, the King's
and the Duke of York's Companies.
Pepys began his diary.

*To My Honored Friend, Sir Rob-
bert Howard* and *Astraea Redux*
published (June).

1661
Cowley's *THE CUTTER OF
COLEMAN STREET.*
D'Avenant's *THE SIEGE OF
RHODES* (e x p a n d e d to two
parts.)

*To His Sacred Majesty, A Pane-
gyric on His Coronation* published
(April).

1662
Charter granted to the Royal
Society.

Publication of *To My Lord Chan-
cellor* (January 1) and *To My*

*Honored Friend, Dr. Charleton* (September\*).
Elected a Fellow of the Royal Society (November 19).

**1663**
Tuke's *THE ADVENTURES OF FIVE HOURS.*

*THE WILD GALLANT* (Vere Street, February 5).
Married Lady Elizabeth Howard (December 1).

**1664**
Sir John Vanbrugh born.
Etherege's *THE COMICAL RE-VENGE.*

*THE INDIAN QUEEN,* with Sir Robert Howard (Bridges Street, January 25).
*THE RIVAL LADIES* (Bridges Street, June).

**1665**
Second Dutch War began (ended 1667).
Great Plague.
Orrery's *MUSTAPHA.*

*THE INDIAN EMPEROR, OR THE CONQUEST OF MEXICO BY THE SPANIARDS* (Bridges Street, April).

**1666**
Fire of London.
Death of James Shirley.

Eldest son, Charles, born (August 27).

**1667**
Jonathan Swift born.
Milton's *Paradise Lost* published.
Sprat's *The History of the Royal Society* published.

*Annus Mirabilis* published (January).
*SECRET LOVE, OR THE MAIDEN QUEEN* (Bridges Street, March 2).
*SIR MARTIN MAR-ALL, OR THE FEIGNED INNOCENCE* (Lincoln's Inn Fields, August 15).
*THE TEMPEST, OR THE EN-CHANTED ISLAND,* with D'Ave-nant (Lincoln's Inn Fields, November 7).

**1668**
Death of D'Avenant.
Shadwell's *THE SULLEN LOV-ERS.*
Etherege's *SHE WOULD IF SHE COULD.*

Second son, John, born.
Appointed Poet Laureate (April).
*An Essay of Dramatick Poesie* published (May or June).
*AN EVENING'S LOVE, OR THE MOCK ASTROLOGER* (Bridges Street, June 12).
Awarded honorary M.A. degree (June 17).

**1669**
Pepys terminated his diary.
Susanna Centlivre born.

Third son, Erasmus-Henry, born (May 2).
*TYRANNIC LOVE, OR THE ROYAL MARTYR* (Bridges Street, June 24).

**1670**
William Congreve born.

Appointed Historiographer Royal (July).
*THE CONQUEST OF GRANADA BY THE SPANIARDS,* Part I (Bridges Street, December).

**1671**
Dorset Garden Theatre (Duke's Company) opened.
Colley Cibber born.
Milton's *Paradise Regained* and *Samson Agonistes* published.
*THE REHEARSAL,* by the Duke of Buckingham and others.
Wycherley's *LOVE IN A WOOD.*

*THE CONQUEST OF GRANADA,* Part II (Bridges Street, January).
*MARRIAGE A LA MODE* (Bridges Street, November*).

**1672**
Third Dutch War began (ended 1674).
Joseph Addison born.
Richard Steele born.

*THE ASSIGNATION, OR LOVE IN A NUNNERY* (Lincoln's Inn Fields, November).

**1673**

*AMBOYNA* (Lincoln's Inn Fields, May).

**1674**
New Drury Lane Theatre (King's Company) opened.
Death of Milton.
Nicholas Rowe born.
Thomas Rymer's *Reflections on Aristotle's Treatise of Poesy* (translation of Rapin) published.

**1675**
Wycherley's *THE COUNTRY WIFE.*

*AURENG-ZEBE* (Drury Lane, November 17).

**1676**
Etherege's *THE MAN OF MODE.*
Otway's *DON CARLOS.*

*Mac Flecknoe* written (July or later).

Shadwell's *THE VIRTUOSO*.
Wycherley's *THE PLAIN DEALER*.

**1677**
Aphra Behn's *THE ROVER*.
Lee's *THE RIVAL QUEENS*.
Rymer's *Tragedies of the Last Age Considered* published.

*THE STATE OF INNOCENCE AND FALL OF MAN* published (February).
*ALL FOR LOVE, OR THE WORLD WELL LOST* (Drury Lane, December 12).

**1678**
Popish Plot.
George Farquhar born.
Bunyan's *Pilgrim's Progress* (Part I) published.

*THE KIND KEEPER, OR MR. LIMBERHAM* (Dorset Garden, March 11).
*OEDIPUS*, with Nathaniel Lee (Dorset Garden, September*).

**1679**
Exclusion Bill introduced.
Death of Thomas Hobbes.
Death of Roger Boyle, Earl of Orrery.
Charles Johnson born.

*TROILUS AND CRESSIDA, OR TRUTH FOUND TOO LATE* (Dorset Garden, April*).
Beaten by hired thugs in Rose Alley on the night of December 18.

**1680**
Death of Samuel Butler.
Death of John Wilmot, Earl of Rochester.
Lee's *LUCIUS JUNIUS BRUTUS*.
Otway's *THE ORPHAN*.

*Ovid's Epistles* published (February).
*THE SPANISH FRIAR, OR THE DOUBLE DISCOVERY* (Dorset Garden, November 1*).

**1681**
Charles II dissolved Parliament at Oxford.
Tate's adaptation of *KING LEAR*.

Publication of *His Majesty's Declaration Defended* (June) and *Absalom and Achitophel*, Part I (November).

**1682**
The King's and the Duke of York's Companies merged into the United Company.
Otway's *VENICE PRESERVED*.

Publication of *The Medal* (March), *Mac Flecknoe* (October), *Absalom and Achitophel*, Part II (November), and *Religio Laici* (November).
*THE DUKE OF GUISE*, with Lee (Drury Lane, November 28).

**1683**
Rye House Plot.
Death of Thomas Killigrew.

Publication of *Vindication of the Duke of Guise* (April*) and trans-

Crowne's *CITY POLITIQUES.*

1684

1685
Death of Charles II; accession of James II.
Revocation of the Edict of Nantes.
The Duke of Monmouth's Rebellion.
Death of Otway.
John Gay born.
Crowne's *SIR COURTLY NICE.*

1686

1687
Death of the Duke of Buckingham.
Newton's *Principia* published.

1688
The Revolution.
Alexander Pope born.
Shadwell's *THE SQUIRE OF ALSATIA.*

1689
The War of the League of Augsburg began (ended 1697).
Toleration Act.
Death of Aphra Behn.
Shadwell made Poet Laureate.
Shadwell's *BURY FAIR.*

1690
Battle of the Boyne.
Locke's *Two Treatises of Government* and *An Essay Concerning Human Understanding* published.

lation of *Plutarch's Lives* (April or May).

Publication of *Miscellany Poems* (February), translation of Maimbourg's *History of the League* (July), and *To the Memory of Mr. Oldham.*

Publication of *Sylvae* (January), *Threnodia Augustalis* (March), and *To the Pious Memory of Mrs. Anne Killigrew* (November). *ALBION AND ALBANIUS* (Dorset Garden, June 3).
Became a Roman Catholic.

*A Defence of the Papers Written by the Late King of Blessed Memory and Duchess of York* published (July).

*The Hind and the Panther* published (May).
*A Song for St. Cecilia's Day, 1687* (November 22).

Publication of *Britannia Rediviva* (June) and translation of Bouhours's *Life of St. Francis Xavier* (July).

*DON SEBASTIAN, KING OF PORTUGAL* (Drury Lane, December 4).

*AMPHITRYON, OR THE TWO SOSIAS,* with music by Henry Purcell (Drury Lane, October 21).

1691
Death of Etherege.*
Langbaine's *An Account of the English Dramatic Poets* published.

*KING ARTHUR, OR THE BRITISH WORTHY*, with music by Purcell (Dorset Garden, May).

1692
Death of Lee.
Death of Shadwell.
Tate made Poet Laureate.

Publication of *Eleonora* (March) and *The Satires of Juvenal and Persius* (October).
*CLEOMENES, THE SPARTAN HERO* (Drury Lane, April).

1693
George Lillo born.*
Rymer's *A Short View of Tragedy* published.
Congreve's *THE OLD BACHELOR*.

Publication of *Examen Poeticum* (July) and *To My Dear Friend, Mr. Congreve* (December).

1694
Death of Queen Mary.
Southerne's *THE FATAL MARRIAGE*.

*LOVE TRIUMPHANT, OR NATURE WILL PREVAIL* (Drury Lane, January).
*The Annual Miscellany, for the Year 1694* published (June).

1695
Group of actors led by Thomas Betterton left Drury Lane and established a new company at Lincoln's Inn Fields.
Congreve's *LOVE FOR LOVE*.
Southerne's *OROONOKO*.

Translation of Du Fresnoy's *Art of Painting* published (July).

1696
Cibber's *LOVE'S LAST SHIFT*.
Vanbrugh's *THE RELAPSE*.

*An Ode on the Death of Mr. Henry Purcell* published (June*).

1697
Treaty of Ryswick ended the War of the League of Augsburg.
Charles Macklin born.
Congreve's *THE MOURNING BRIDE*.
Vanbrugh's *THE PROVOKED WIFE*.

Translation of Virgil published (August).
*Alexander's Feast* (November 22).

1698
Collier controversy started with the publication of *A Short View of the Immorality and Profaneness of the English Stage*.

1699
Farquhar's *THE CONSTANT COUPLE.*

1700
Blackmore's *Satire against Wit* published.
Congreve's *THE WAY OF THE WORLD.*

*Fables Ancient and Modern* published (March).
Died in London, May 1.

1701
Act of Settlement.
War of the Spanish Succession began (ended 1713).
Death of James II.
Rowe's *TAMERLANE.*
Steele's *THE FUNERAL.*

1702
Death of William III; accession of Anne.
*The Daily Courant* began publication.
Cibber's *SHE WOULD AND SHE WOULD NOT.*

1703
Death of Samuel Pepys.
Rowe's *THE FAIR PENITENT.*

1704
Capture of Gibraltar; Battle of Blenheim.
Defoe's *The Review* began publication (1704–1713).
Swift's *A Tale of a Tub* and *The Battle of the Books* published.
Cibber's *THE CARELESS HUSBAND.*

1705
Haymarket Theatre opened.
Steele's *THE TENDER HUSBAND.*

1706
Battle of Ramillies.
Farquhar's *THE RECRUITING OFFICER.*

1707
Union of Scotland and England.
Death of Farquhar.

Henry Fielding born.
Farquhar's *THE BEAUX'
STRATAGEM.*

1708
Downes's *Roscius Anglicanus* published.

1709
Samuel Johnson born.
Rowe's edition of Shakespeare published.
*The Tatler* began publication (1709–1711).
Centlivre's *THE BUSY BODY.*

1711
Shaftesbury's *Characteristics* published.
*The Spectator* began publication (1711–1712).
Pope's *An Essay on Criticism* published.

1713
Treaty of Utrecht ended the War of the Spanish Succession.
Addison's *CATO.*

1714
Death of Anne; accession of George I.
Steele became Governor of Drury Lane.
John Rich assumed management of Lincoln's Inn Fields.
Centlivre's *THE WONDER: A WOMAN KEEPS A SECRET.*
Rowe's *JANE SHORE.*

1715
Jacobite Rebellion.
Death of Tate.
Rowe made Poet Laureate.
Death of Wycherley.

1716
Addison's *THE DRUMMER.*

1717
David Garrick born.
Cibber's *THE NON-JUROR.*

Gay, P o p e, and Arbuthnot's
*THREE HOURS AFTER MAR-
RIAGE.*

1718
Death of Rowe.
Centlivre's *A BOLD STROKE
FOR A WIFE.*

1719
Death of Addison.
Defoe's *Robinson Crusoe* pub-
lished.
Young's *BUSIRIS, KING OF
EGYPT.*

1720
South Sea Bubble.
Samuel Foote born.
Steele suspended from the Gover-
norship of Drury Lane (restored
1721).
Little Theatre in the Haymarket
opened.
Steele's *The Theatre* (periodical)
published.
Hughes's *THE SIEGE OF DA-
MASCUS.*

1721
Walpole became first Minister.

1722
Steele's *THE C O N S C I O U S
LOVERS.*

1723
Death of Susanna Centlivre.
Death of D'Urfey.

1725
Pope's edition of Shakespeare
published.

1726
Death of Jeremy Collier.
Death of Vanbrugh.
Law's *Unlawfulness of Stage En-
tertainments* published.
Swift's *Gulliver's Travels* pub-
lished.

1727
Death of George I; accession of

George II.
Death of Sir Isaac Newton.
Arthur Murphy born.

1728
Pope's *The Dunciad* (first version) published.
Cibber's *THE PROVOKED HUSBAND* (expansion of Vanbrugh's fragment *A JOURNEY TO LONDON*).
Gay's *THE BEGGAR'S OPERA*.

1729
Goodman's Fields Theatre opened.
Death of Congreve.
Death of Steele.
Edmund Burke born.

1730
Cibber made Poet Laureate.
Oliver Goldsmith born.
Thomson's *The Seasons* published.
Fielding's *THE AUTHOR'S FARCE*.
Fielding's *TOM THUMB* (revised as *THE TRAGEDY OF TRAGEDIES*, 1731).

1731
Death of Defoe.
Fielding's *THE GRUB-STREET OPERA*.
Lillo's *THE LONDON MERCHANT*.

1732
Covent Garden Theatre opened.
Death of Gay.
George Colman the elder born.
Fielding's *THE COVENT GARDEN TRAGEDY*.
Fielding's *THE MODERN HUSBAND*.
Charles Johnson's *CAELIA*.

1733
Pope's *An Essay on Man* (Epistles I–III) published (Epistle **IV**, 1734).

1734
Death of Dennis.
*The Prompter* began publication
(1734–1736).
Theobald's edition of Shakes-
peare published.
Fielding's *DON QUIXOTE IN
ENGLAND.*

1736
Fielding led the "Great Mogul's
Company of Comedians" at the
Little Theatre in the Haymarket
(1736–1737).
Fielding's *PASQUIN.*
Lillo's *FATAL CURIOSITY.*

1737
The Stage Licensing Act.
Dodsley's *THE KING AND THE
MILLER OF MANSFIELD.*
Fielding's *THE HISTORICAL
REGISTER FOR THE YEAR
1736.*